Marketin

Marketing Simulation

A Decision Support System Approach

Third Edition

Ronald F. Bush
The University of West Florida

Alvin C. Burns
Louisiana State University

HarperCollinsPublishers

Sponsoring Editor: Suzy Spivey
Project Editor: Thomas R. Farrell
Cover Design: Ron Slanina
Production Administrator: Paula Keller
Printer and Binder: Courier Stoughton, Inc.
Cover Printer: Lynn Art Offset Corporation

Marketing Simulation: *A Decision Support System Approach,* Third Edition

Copyright ©1991 by HarperCollins Publishers Inc.

All rights reserved. Printed in the United States of America. No part of this book may be used or reproduced in any manner whatsoever without written permission, except in the case of brief quotations embodied in critical articles and reviews. For information address HarperCollins Publishers Inc., 10 East 53rd Street, New York, NY 10022.

Library of Congress Cataloging-in-Publication Data

Bush, Ronald F.
    Marketing simulation : a decision support system approach / Ronald
F. Bush, Alvin C. Burns. -- 3rd ed.
      p.   cm.
   Rev. ed. of: Marketing simulation / Bob Brobst, Ronald F. Bush.
2nd ed. c1983.
   Includes index.
   ISBN 0-06-361075-2
   1. Marketing--Simulation methods. 2. Marketing--Management-
-Simulation methods.   I. Burns, Alvin C. II. Brobst, Bob.
Marketing simulation. III. Title.
HF5415.B678   1990   90-20188
                                        CIP

90 91 92 93   9 8 7 6 5 4 3 2 1

Contents

Preface ix

Chapter 1 Introduction to Marketing Simulation 1

Why Simulate Marketing Decisions? 2
Marketing Simulation: The Setting 2
    Your DSS Disk: DIS and DAT 3
    Changing Environments 4
    The Start-Up Position 5
Getting Started 5
    An Overview of the Simulation Procedure 5
    Organizing Your Team 7
    Establish Communication 9
    Establish Responsibility Centers 9
    Set Up a System for Review and Control 9
    Consistent Effort Is Effective 10
    Information from Former Students 10
    Setting Company Objectives 11
    Understanding Printouts and Forms 11
How to Operate Your Student DSS Disk 15
Preliminaries: Copying BASIC onto Your DSS Disk 15
Getting into the DSS Program 16
Running DIS 16
Moving to DAT from DIS 18
Loading DAT Without Using DSS 18
Running DAT 19
The Master Menu: Accessing the Tools 19
Using the Tools 20
Practicing with DIS and DAT 20

Chapter 2 The Industry and Your Company 21

The Industry 21
Your Company 21
    Your Income Statement 21
    Your Balance Sheet 23

Chapter 3 Marketing Strategy 25

The Meaning of Marketing Strategy 25
Determining Your Company's Marketing Strategy 26
Market Segmentation 27
    Market Segmentation in Marketing Simulation 28
Product Strategy 29
    Product Strategy in Marketing Simulation 30
    R & D Expenditures 41
Channel Strategy 43
    Channel Strategy in Marketing Simulation 44
Pricing Strategy 47
    Pricing Objectives 47
    Pricing Strategies: Discount, Premium, and At the Market 47
    Pricing Strategy in Marketing Simulation 48
Promotion Strategy 51
Determining the Promotion Budget 52
    Promotion Strategy in Marketing Simulation 54

Chapter 4 Marketing Research 57

Quarterly Sales Forecast 58
Competitive-Dealer Studies 58
Competitive-Promotion Studies 59
Study of Competitors' Sales Force Size 60
Studies of Competitors' R & D 60
Consumer Preference Studies 61

Chapter 5 Evaluating Your Performance 63

Measures of Effectiveness 64
    Measures of Effectiveness in Marketing Simulation 64
Measures of Efficiency 65
    Measures of Efficiency in Marketing Simulation 66
The Decision Analysis Tools 67
    How to Operate Your DAT 71
    Your Practice Data Set 71
    How to Share the Current Data Base with Other Team Members 71

Appendix A Understanding Your Income Statement and Sources and Uses of Funds Form 73

The Income Statement 73
    Sales 74
    Cost of Sales 74
    Operating Expenses 75
    Income and Taxes 76
The Sources and Uses of Funds Form 76

Appendix B Completing Your Decision Forms 79

The Marketing Research Request Form 79
The Management Decision Form 80

Appendix C Blank Forms 83

Appendix D Sample Printouts 121

Appendix E Sample Tests 129

Appendix F Installing BASIC on Your DSS Disk 139

Index 141

Preface

The field of marketing education has changed dramatically with the widespread adoption of the microcomputer. There has been a marked increase in computer availability at colleges and universities, and more and more software is available for our students' use in learning about marketing. While we can expect even more significant changes in computer-assisted education in the near future, today's typical marketing student is computer literate or, at the very least, has some knowledge of basic computer operation. This fact, coupled with the recommendation from the American Assembly of Collegiate Schools of Business (AACSB) to provide more hands-on computer experiences in the classroom, led to the changes we have incorporated in the third edition of **Marketing Simulation**.

Marketing Simulation is a microcomputer-based simulation designed to aid students in learning how to analyze market information in order to plan and evaluate marketing strategy. Students compete with each other in teams; each team represents a company within the television industry. Key decisions to be made are

> **Market segment selection**
> **Choice of appropriate TV models**
> **Production scheduling**
> **Pricing**
> **Selection of types and numbers of retail distribution outlets**
> **Selection of types and amounts to be spent on various**
> > **forms of promotion including advertising, sales**
> > **promotion and personal sales force**
> **R&D expenditures**
> **Marketing research information**

A major improvement in the third edition of **Marketing Simulation** is that the simulation is now totally operated by the microcomputer. Student teams select one disk to serve as the Team DSS Disk. They enter their decisions on that disk and submit it to the instructor. The team decisions are inputted into a computer program designed to simulate market conditions for one quarter of business activity. Instructors simply load in all team disks and execute the simulation program which records all the appropriate results (income statements, balance sheets, etc.) on each Team DSS Disk. The instructor then returns the disks to the student teams and they may view the results on their computer screen or print a hard copy.

The student teams receive feedback on the quality of their marketing decisions in the form of standard financial statements and other market information. After examining their results, student teams make decisions for the next period of simulated business activity and, once again, submit the Team DSS disk to the instructor. This procedure continues until the instructor announces that the simulation has ended. Administrative time is minimal.

A second improvement in this edition of **Marketing Simulation** lies in providing an enriching experience for students by encouraging them to interact with the microcomputer. A Decision Support System (DSS) was designed to accompany the third edition. The DSS is contained on the Student DSS Disk which accompanies this book. The DSS is composed of two routines: The Decision Input System (DIS) and Decision Analysis Tools (DAT). These are explained among the special features of **Marketing Simulation** listed below.

1. **Decision Support System (DSS) Aspects.** A decision support system aids managers in gathering and organizing information so that it may be used as an aid in managerial decision-making. A Decision Support System approach is now incorporated to facilitate student team decision making. The DSS is composed of two sets of programs which have different functions:

    Decision Input System (DIS). The program DIS takes students step-by-step through the decision specification process allowing them to enter, transmit and receive information. It assists them in making marketing management and marketing research decisions each period and writes their decisions onto a file to be read by the program on the Instructor's Disk when batch-run. It also allows students to review their printouts on a PC screen or print them on a printer.

    Decision Analysis Tools (DAT). We have provided the Student DSS Disk with an extensive set of planning and analysis tools using Lotus 1–2–3 templates. Everything is preprogrammed: students follow the menus to access the historical database which is updated with each period's results each time the instructor makes a simulation run. DAT provides graphical presentations of the database as well as routines that do analyses such as break-even or cash flow.

2. **Completely "Disk-Driven."** Everything is done with computer files: students hand in their decisions on their Team DSS Disk and the instructor returns the disk after each period's run. There is no need for paper decision forms or printouts to be exchanged between instructor and student teams. Teams may print out their results (income statement, balance sheet, marketing research study results,

Preface xi

etc.) at their convenience, and the instructor may do the same. Also, students and the instructor may view the results directly on their computer's screen.

3. **Updated and Expanded Marketing Decision Variables.** Although the addition of the DSS is a major change, at the request of adopters of the first and second editions, we have left the basics of the simulation the same. However, we have **updated the TV models** in keeping with trends in the industry and we have **added a sales force variable.** Student teams may now vary the size of the sales force that markets to the retail channel. Student teams receiving technological breakthroughs as a result of R & D expenditures will receive **R & D messages** telling them the nature of the breakthrough.

4. **Preprogrammed Marketing Environments.** We have **included a set of preprogrammed environments on the Instructor's Disk.** By simply selecting an environment from a menu, an instructor can easily change the simulation parameters. Thus, an instructor could have two totally different marketing environments between two industries in the same class and may easily change the nature of the simulation between terms or semesters. These environments are fully explained in the Instructor's Manual.

5. **Completely "PC" Based.** Marketing Simulation, Third Edition, has been designed for use on any IBM or IBM-compatible personal computer with 640K memory. Although this program was designed and tested in an IBM environment, it may run on any DOS-based computer since the program is written in BASIC.

6. **Entirely Menu-Operated.** Everything on the Student DSS Disk and the Instructor Disk is handled by menus. All you and your students need to do is select the number of the item of the routine you wish to perform. Prompts in the program direct the user on what to do when.

7. **Built-in Safeguards.** We have programmed **Marketing Simulation** so it will beep and/or notify you of when to put disks in, take them out, or respond to menu instructions. It has built-in checks to make sure procedures are followed correctly.

TO THE STUDENT

Your Decision Support System is already programmed on your Student DSS Disk, packaged with this book. A DSS aids managers in transmitting information, such as marketing decisions, to appropriate members of the organization, as well as gathering, sorting, editing, and storing information that may be retrieved for analysis in order to make additional decisions. Your DSS accomplishes both of these objectives. First, in order for you to easily transmit information, we have programmed a set of screens that allows you to enter your marketing management decisions. When you load in your Student DSS Disk you will see a menu of these screens for you to enter your team members' names; enter your marketing management decisions; enter requests for marketing research studies; and so on. Collectively, we refer to this part of your DSS as the Decision Input System (DIS). DIS allows you totally to run your television company via your microcomputer.

An option on your menu allows you to exit the DIS and enter into another set of Lotus 1-2-3-based programs, which allows for the second function of a DSS—gathering, sorting, editing, storing, and allowing for the retrieval of information. We refer to this part of the DSS as the Decision Analysis Tools (DAT) because it contains "tools" to aid you in making decisions such as break-even analysis, techniques for forecasting sales, and graphical analyses of historical data. DAT is automatically updated with new data each time your instructor runs the simulation, and you may retrieve these data for analysis by simply selecting the DAT menu item.

REQUIREMENTS

Student Background

At least one introductory course in accounting is necessary. Students should also have some basic knowledge in the operation of a microcomputer. No programming is required; the software is totally menu-driven.

WARNING: Some students will have the necessary computer background to attempt to examine the computer code on their Student DSS Disk. You should be forewarned that your Student DSS Disk contains no information that could help you understand the simulation parameters or give you an advantage over other teams with whom you are competing. Therefore, be advised that if you do examine the code on the Student DSS Disk, you have nothing to gain and you may ruin your disk.

Hardware

This simulation was designed and tested on IBM and IBM-compatible microcomputers. However, since the simulation is written in BASIC, by copying your machine's BASIC onto your Student DSS Disk, the simulation may run on virtually any DOS-based computer. The program requires 640K of memory.

Software

You will need to copy your computer's version of BASIC onto the Student DSS Disk that accompanies this book. This disk is necessary for students to input their decisions (the DIS), and also serves as the medium for the simulation's output. This same Student DSS Disk also houses the DAT. Instructions for copying BASIC onto your Student DSS Disk are in Appendix F.

You will also need Lotus 1-2-3 or another Lotus-compatible spreadsheet program in order to access the DAT part of the DSS. If you do not have Lotus 1-2-3, you will still be able to run the simulation, but you will not have access to DAT. Instructions for running DAT are provided at the end of Chapter 1.

ESPECIALLY FOR THE INSTRUCTOR

Adopters of this simulation should receive a copy of the student manual

Ronald F. Bush
Alvin C. Burns

Chapter 1
Introduction to Marketing Simulation

Marketing Simulation will introduce you to an exciting learning experience that should increase your decision-making abilities in business and provide exposure to a "real-world" competitive marketing environment while you are studying marketing. **Marketing Simulation** allows you to analyze market conditions and make decisions as if you were making marketing decisions in the real world. Each time you make a set of decisions you will receive an income statement, a balance sheet, and other information. You will also be aided in your decision-making task by a **Decision Support System (DSS)**. The DSS diskette, provided with this volume, will give you important data that will enhance your decision-making capabilities.

The setting for your simulation is the television industry. You and your fellow students make up the management team responsible for the marketing decisions in a television company that manufactures and markets TV sets. Your firm will compete with up to as many as four other companies. (Your instructor will tell you how many other firms are involved in the competition.) Your decisions involve determining:

1. what types of television sets to produce and in what quantities to produce them;
2. through what types and quantity of channel members to distribute your sets;
3. what prices to charge your dealers for your sets;
4. how much to spend on various forms of promotion including determining the size of your sales force;
5. what kinds of marketing research reports to buy to aid you in your decision making; and
6. how much to invest in R & D.

This book gives you all the information you need to conduct this simulation but you must study it carefully.

WHY SIMULATE MARKETING DECISIONS?

There is no substitute for real-world experience when it comes to learning about the nature and function of business. Some students have some business experience or perhaps may be enrolled in a co-operative educational program. The fact is, however, that few students have business experience, and of those who do, very few have been in positions where they had the opportunity to make decisions involving all the various business functions. This situation represents a "gap" in business education—a gap between classroom knowledge and real-world application. Unfortunately, it is not practical or feasible to allow each student of business to actually operate a company for a specified time. Therefore, many innovative educators have utilized simulations to help fill the gap. Simulation was first used in business education in the 1950s and has since become recognized as an effective teaching device. Simulations are now not only used in colleges and universities and in executive training programs, they are also used in business and government to help determine optimal decisions given very complex environments. Simulations have both educational and practical value. The primary value of simulations is that they allow you to develop your skills in an area that is vital to all managerial situations—decision making. Through simulation you will get as close to actual business experience—at the decision-making level—as you possibly can without leaving your classroom.

You should be aware that this simulation deals primarily with marketing variables—sales forecasting and product selection, pricing, distribution, and promotion. Other simulations may emphasize different variables. A finance simulation, for example, would probably emphasize such variables as cash flow, investment of excess cash, and sources and cost of capital. While the operation of a business firm involves decisions in many areas, **Marketing Simulation** emphasizes the *marketing* decision variables. Many of these other business variables are programmed to respond to your marketing decisions automatically. For example, you will automatically be given a loan if you run out of cash and you will not be allowed to invest your excess cash. You must compete on the basis of the marketing variables in **Marketing Simulation**.

MARKETING SIMULATION: THE SETTING

To get you started, you may assume that you and your teammates have just taken over the management of a firm that manufactures and markets television sets. You have very limited information about the former operation of your firm. You will have a set of "start-up" data in the form of a beginning income statement and balance sheet, and other information. This start-up information is provided in this book. Also, the set of decisions that led to these results is provided in this chapter. As already noted, the number of competitors in your industry will be determined by your instructor. However, a maximum of only five firms is allowed in any industry. Therefore, you may not have more than four competitors.

You and your teammates will compete with the other firms in your industry by periodically making a set of decisions (i.e., determining the types of TV models to produce, the price of your TVs, methods of promoting your TVs, and the selection of dealers to distribute your TVs, etc.) Each set of decisions will be recorded on a management decision form. Your instructor has a choice as to how you will actually enter your decisions: entering your decisions on the DSS disk provided with this book on a microcomputer, or on copies of blank forms provided for you in Appendix C. In either case, after you make your decisions, you will turn in your decisions to your instructor, who will submit your decisions to be analyzed by a computer program designed to simulate actual business activity in your industry. Each decision period simulates one quarter of business activity. If you are entering decisions on your DSS disk, your instructor will return the DSS disk and you will be able to view your results on your computer screen and/or print out your firm's balance sheet, income statement, and other information. Your DSS disk will also contain updated information about your firm and industry that will aid you in making future decisions. Or, if you've turned in your decisions on one of the paper forms provided, your instructor will return a set of printouts to you.

Your Student DSS Disk: DIS and DAT

You will soon enter the business world and become a manager of the future. That means that you will probably be involved with a fast-paced, computer-driven, information-saturated world of management decisions. Not only will you have computer technology at your command, but you will have access to very extensive pools of information about your company, competitors, customers, and trends in your industry. Managers of the future will have ready-made, menu-driven, computerized decision support systems at their fingertips. We have endeavored to make this version of **Marketing Simulation** as close to this picture of the future as possible.

You have been provided with a computer disk along with this manual. We refer to it as the **Student DSS (Decision Support System Disk)** throughout. Actually, there are two parts to your DSS disk. One part is the **Decision Input System**, which we refer to as DIS. The DIS part of your DSS disk contains programs for setting up your industry according to your instructor's directions, making marketing research study requests, and making marketing decisions such as model, price, and promotion. The DIS operates with BASIC computer language, which you will have to put on your DSS disk. Most likely, your instructor will tell you how to copy BASIC onto your DSS disk. He or she may have you use the BASIC available in you computer laboratory, or may suggest other ways for you accomplish this. Otherwise, there are instructions in Appendix F for copying your computer's BASIC onto your Student DSS disk.

The other part of your DSS disk contains several **Decision Analysis Tools,** so we refer to this part as DAT. These routines are written to be used with Lotus 1−2−3 (Version 2.0 or later), and you must first load Lotus 1−2−3 on your computer before the DAT routines will run. Here, you do not need to copy Lotus 1−2−3 onto your DSS disk: all you need do is to have Lotus 1−2−3 running. (Please note: Many Lotus 1−2−3 competitor spreadsheet programs will run DAT, so if you have some other program, DAT *may* run on it. Try it or ask your Instructor about what to use.) We review the DAT part of your DSS disk in Chapter 5, and we describe all of the analytical tools at appropriate places in Chapter 3. Instructions on loading DAT are at the end of this chapter; instructions on using DAT are in Chapter 5.

Your DAT is very important. You should use it to help you analyze the tremendous stock of information that **Marketing Simulation** will generate with each quarter of simulated business activity. To aid you in getting familiar with your DAT, two years of practice data has been generated and placed on your disk. We have created a fictitious company, company X-1, to allow you to examine its data over the past eight quarters. You should use this data to help you prepare for the type of data that will be provided to you on your DAT as you actually compete in **Marketing Simulation**.

In summary, you have a **Student Decision Support System (DSS)** disk. It contains:

DIS—Decision Input System

The purpose of the DIS is to allow you to enter your decisions directly onto you DSS disk. It will not run until you have loaded BASIC. Your instructor will tell you how to do this or you may follow the instructions in Appendix F.

DAT—Decision Analysis Tools

The purpose of the DAT is to provide you with some tools such as break-even analysis, a cash-flow model, forecasting models, and graphs to help you analyze information to aid your decision making. Instructions on loading DAT are at the end of this chapter; instructions on using DAT are in Chapter 5.

If your instructor prefers that you enter your decisions on paper forms, your DSS disk will not be of much use. In this event, you will use the blank forms in Appendix C to enter your decision. Even in this case, you should try to use some of the techniques just mentioned to help your decision making. You simply will not have the benefit of a computerized DSS.

Changing Environments

As you have probably already learned, the environment is constantly changing and environmental change is very significant in marketing. When fuel prices escalated during the 1970s it totally changed the market demand for automobiles. During the 1980s consumers drastically changed their desires for foods, drink, and leisure-time activities due to a new concern for their health and appearance. The environment will continue to change during the 1990s and this will affect marketing firms. Your instructor has the ability to select various environments for this simulation as well. Please note that the eight quarters of practice data for firm X-1 provided for you on your DSS disk are there for the purpose of helping you to learn how to use your DIS and DAT. You should realize that any relationships you may observe between marketing decisions and market response may be misleading in the new environment your instructor will select for your actual competition in **Marketing Simulation**.

Once you begin the actual simulation, your DSS disk will automatically be updated with new data that is relevant to the market environment. Like all good marketing managers you should carefully monitor this information. Firms that are sensitive to their environment and that design a marketing mix that is well suited to their environment are much more likely to outperform their competition.

The Start-Up Position

All teams will start the simulation in an equal position. All have identical income statements, balance sheets, market shares, and so on. You may assume that a previous, "fictitious" management made the set of decisions shown in Table 1.1, Former Management Decisions. (Note that Table 1.1 is a copy of the Management Decision Form that you will fill out in order to make your firm's decisions). This set of decisions resulted in the income statement and balance sheet that are shown in Chapter 2 in Tables 2.1 and 2.2, respectively.

By examining Table 1.2, the Marketing Research Request Form (Form 2 in Appendix C), you will see that former management did not request any marketing research information before they left the firm. However, this form is shown to you at this point so that you may familiarize yourself with it. This is the first form your team will have to complete because you will be given the opportunity to purchase marketing research information prior to making your first management decision by completing the management decision form (Form 3 in Appendix C). That is, you will be given the opportunity to ask for marketing research information prior to making your first set of actual decisions for the first quarter of simulation.

GETTING STARTED

The following paragraphs should help you take over the management of your firm. Included is an overview of the simulation procedure. Also, discussions are provided on how to organize your management team, setting objectives for your firm, and the forms you will work with while competing in **Marketing Simulation**.

As we noted earlier, the DIS part of your DSS disk requires BASIC, and the DAT part of it requires Lotus 1-2-3. Your instructor will give you directions on how to copy BASIC onto your DSS disk or you may follow the instructions in Appendix F. Instructions on how to load Lotus 1-2-3 to operate the DAT part of your DSS disk are at the end of this chapter.

An Overview of the Simulation Procedure

At this point you may find it helpful to get an idea of the basic procedure you will undertake while competing in **Marketing Simulation**. The following steps will give you a concise conceptual overview of the procedure you should follow. (Note: the following assumes your instructor will have you enter your decisions on your DSS disk. If not, you will turn in your decisions on the blank forms provided in Appendix C and your instructor will return your printouts to you.)

TABLE 1.1
MANAGEMENT DECISION FORM

Year: ____   Industry (Letter): _____

Quarter: ____   Company (Number): _____

		Model 1	Model 2	Model 3	Model 4
1.	Model Code:	B	G	K	P
2.	Price:	125	160	250	825
3.	Units Produced:	740	1,125	1,800	450
4.	TV Advertising (000):	5	5	5	5
5.	Magazine Advertising (000):	5	5	5	5
6.	Newspaper Advertising (000):	5	5	5	5
7.	Sales Promotion (000):	5	5	5	5

8. Sales Force: 10

9. Research & Development (000): 0

10. Dealer Allocation:

Furniture Store	Specialty Store	Discount Store	Department Store
40	160	80	120

1. Read and study this book in its entirety. Test your understanding of the material in this book by taking the sample test provided for you in Appendix E.
2. Follow the instructions in this book on how to use your Student DSS disk. Study the eight quarters of historical data provided on the disk. *Become familiar with your DSS disk before you actually start the simulation.* We provide step-by-step instructions for operating your DSS disk at the end of this chapter.
3. Your instructor will assign you to a team. Your firm will also be assigned an identifying code: an industry letter and company number. Select one of your team member's disks to serve as the **Team DSS Disk,** which will always be given to the instructor with each quarter's decisions and returned to your team with the results. Your instructor will collect

your Team DSS disk. He/she will erase all of the practice X-1 data and set your disk to start the simulation.
4. Organize your team for effective decision making over the course of the simulation. Follow the guidelines suggested in the following section of this chapter.
5. Determine what marketing research information you need to aid you in making the first set of marketing management decisions. Your instructor will tell you when you are ready to enter your request for marketing research. Since this request is made prior to the actual start of the simulation, it will be assigned a designation of Year 1, Quarter 0. Complete the Marketing Research Request on your Team DSS disk and give that disk to your instructor. Even if you decide not to buy any research, you must turn in your Team DSS disk at this time. You must *always* give your team disk to your instructor for each period of simulation play. Even if you decide not to change any of your decisions from one quarter to the next, you must re-enter those same decisions and give your disk to your instructor. Always properly label and back up your disks.
6. Your instructor will return your Team DSS disk with the marketing research information you requested, if any. Study and use this information to make your first set of marketing management decisions by entering these decisions on your Team DSS disk, the Management Decision Form, for your first simulation decision: Year 1, Quarter 1.
7. When you submit your decisions to your instructor for the Year 1, Quarter 1 decision, you may also want to submit another request for marketing research. This will enable you to receive research information in order to aid you in making the Year 1, Quarter 2 management decision.
8. After you submit completed forms 2 and 3 on your Team DSS disk to your instructor, she or he will return the disk to you so that you may see the results of the simulation. By selecting the Print Company Reports option, you may view your results on screen or print a hard copy. You will receive an income statement, balance sheet, and sales information, which will enable you to assess your competitive standing. Also, if you remembered to purchase marketing research information at the time you submitted your management decisions you will be given the information you requested. Finally, your DSS disk will be updated. This current information will be available to use your DAT to aid you in analyzing and revising your management decisions, if necessary, so that you may submit a new set of decisions.
9. This process repeats itself until your instructor informs you that the simulation competition has ended.

Organizing Your Team

By this time in your college career you've probably experienced working on group projects. If so, you've learned the importance of team organization. Team Organization is very important in **Marketing**

TABLE 1.2
MARKETING RESEARCH REQUEST FORM

Year: _____   Industry (Letter): _____

Quarter: _____   Company (Number): _____

STUDY		COST	Y or N
1.	Quarterly Sales Forecast by Submarket	$20,000	N
2.	Current Number of Dealers by Company	$ 5,000	N
3.	Current Number of Dealers by Channel Type per Company	$20,000	N
4.	Current Promotion Expenditures by Company	$ 5,000	N
5.	Current Promotion Expenditures by Submarket per Company	$20,000	N
6.	Current Promotion Expenditures/Submarket/Medium/Company	$25,000	N
7.	Sales Force Size by Company	$15,000	N
8.	Cumulative R & D Expenditures by Company	$ 5,000	N
9.	Consumer Preference Study of All Models/Submarket 1	$30,000	N
10.	Consumer Preference Study of All Models/Submarket 2	$30,000	N
11.	Consumer Preference Study of All Models/Submarket 3	$30,000	N
12.	Consumer Preference Study of All Models/Submarket 4	$30,000	N
	Total:		

Simulation. You are about to assume a share of the decision-making responsibility of a marketing executive in a highly competitive industry. Accordingly, you should strive to organize your team in such a way that you get maximum cooperative effort from all members.

Your industry will be designated with a letter and your company with a number by your instructor at the beginning of play. Thus your company may have the designation "A-2," meaning the second company in industry A. In this example, you would compete with companies A-1, A-3, A-4, and A-5. (Of course if there is only one industry in your class it may be designated "A"; if there is another, it may be "B"; and so on.) Since this letter and number combination will be used to identify your company, it is important to remember your company's designation and place it on all forms and disks you use.

Almost without exception, well-organized teams usually perform better than poorly organized ones. In fact, careless errors, often resulting in disastrous consequences, are usually the result of poor team organization. In case you haven't gotten the point by now—devote time and energy to proper organization. Make certain you contribute your fair share and cooperate with all other members. Some suggestions for organizing your team and taking the first steps in **Marketing Simulation** are discussed in the following paragraphs.

Establish Communication

Get fully acquainted and give each other your telephone numbers and addresses. It is important that each team have an effective means of communicating while not in class.

Establish Responsibility Centers

Have you ever noticed being in a team situation and discussing matters that need to be taken care of yet no one was specifically assigned the task of taking care of any of the matters? Recall what happened? Right! Nothing happened and the next time you met you still had the same problems except you had lost valuable time. There is a way to remedy this situation; you must always assign specific responsibilities to individuals. This means that each team will want to make each of its members responsible for a set (or "center") of activities necessary to compete effectively in **Marketing Simulation**. For example, every team should make one member responsible for bringing all the materials and records to class (or to another meeting place) so the team can use them in making decisions. Each decision period, or quarter, will require a number of decisions, and those decisions will require some knowledge of former decisions—usually the most recent one. Make sure your team always has the appropriate records so that you may make the best possible decisions.

Examples of other responsibility centers are team communications, setting objectives, product model selection, sales forecasting and production scheduling decisions, channel choice and dealer allocation, pricing, promotion, marketing research, and DAT analyses. Note that these are only examples. Your company may operate more effectively with other responsibility centers. The important point here is that each team should assign its members specific areas of responsibility. However, this should not be done until everyone is familiar with the basic nature, guidelines, and decision rules of **Marketing Simulation**. (Be sure you take the sample test in Appendix E after you have studied this book.) Once you are familiar with this book you will be in a good position to determine what your responsibility centers will be and which team members should be responsible for them.

Set Up a System for Review and Control

One of the most important management functions is that of control. The best of plans may go astray without a good control system. Control simply means taking a look at how you're performing relative to how you need to be performing. If you're off-target, you need to take corrective action. You cannot properly manage without an adequate control system. In the beginning of the simulation, after responsibilities have been assigned, make certain that everyone understands that the team needs to review everyone's performance at certain intervals. This means that the team should determine the time at which each individual's contribution will be reviewed. Be wary of not doing this; many students have a distaste for evaluating their fellow students and they fail to review their colleagues' performance. This means, of course, that the team does not have a control system. If you are learning to hold responsible management positions you must deal with this issue and you must do it on a regular basis. Every other week during a normal semester or quarter would not be too often. Note also that a review team meeting should not be distasteful to anyone. It should be handled in a professional manner that assesses the extent to which team members are doing their assigned activities. If a team member is not performing "to the standard," a discussion should ensue to determine why and how to best remedy the situation. If this process is started early and is done regularly, you should have a very pleasant and probably successful team experience.

You should try to resolve any problems that arise without calling on your instructor. Even though your instructor will probably know about your problems—whether they are caused by not completing your decision form properly, by overpricing your models, or even by team members not doing their fair share—do not call on him or her without having first made an attempt to resolve them yourselves. Do not procrastinate; problems must be resolved as they are detected. It will be too late to inform your instructor of a problem near the end of the simulation.

Consistent Effort Is Effective

For effective team organization, each member should understand that success requires a consistent level of effort on the part of each individual. Your team should plan meetings on a regular basis throughout the simulation. The meetings will be more lengthy in the beginning, but as play continues, meeting time should decrease. Since **Marketing Simulation** does not lend itself to "cram sessions," well-planned team meetings on a regular basis will be beneficial.

Information from Former Students

You will probably talk with students who have already played **Marketing Simulation** during previous semesters or quarters. Often, in an attempt to be helpful, former students will pass on the marketing strategy that helped them earn profits in **Marketing Simulation**. You should be warned, however, that the computer program in **Marketing Simulation** is "dynamic." As you have been told, your instructor has the ability to change the environments in **Marketing Simulation**. Therefore, the strategy that worked for one team last semester or quarter may be disastrous given the new environment.

By all means, learn what you can from former students. They will have some good ideas about team organization, record keeping, and so on. But, don't be misled into thinking you've discovered the one way to "beat the game"—it doesn't exist. The best way to beat the game is to read this book carefully, follow its suggestions, and think through your decisions before you make them.

Setting Company Objectives

Setting objectives is an important team function. Your team should state objectives (or goals) to be achieved by your company during various stages of the simulation period. Objectives are important because they provide you with some idea of what you wish to achieve. If objectives are set properly, they also serve as a constructive mechanism for helping you determine your strategy—the way you go about achieving objectives.

Consider the following example. Suppose you have determined that your income after taxes for the coming period should be $200,000. You arrived at this objective by stating several other objectives. Market share is anticipated to be 35 percent; gross sales are expected to be $2 million; cost of sales is estimated to be $950,000; and so on. Each of these figures represents an objective that the company must achieve in order to reach the objective of $200,000 in income after taxes. Assume now that the company's activity results in income after taxes of $130,000 instead of the projected $200,000. You will ask, "What happened?" Look back over the other objectives. Were your sales lower than expected? Were your costs greater than expected? The answers to these questions will give you some guidance in revising your decisions for the next quarter of business activity. Without proper objectives you will not have an adequate base for corrective action.

Objectives should be specific and related to a particular quantifiable result of your company's operations (sales, for example). Objectives should also be reasonable. For example, no one will ever get 100 percent of the market unless one has a monopoly. Also, your objectives should be flexible—change them if you believe you have set them either too high or too low. The objectives you set will become more useful the longer you play **Marketing Simulation**. Do not be discouraged if you feel at a loss in the beginning. Remember, you have yet to gain "experience" in "your" industry. Keep working and you will learn the important role objectives play in the operation of a business firm.

You are provided with an Objectives and Planning Form (Form 1) in Appendix C. This gives you a format for recording your objectives and your plans for achieving them—your strategies and tactics. You should keep an accurate record of your objectives on this form, since it will guide your decision making. You should also keep a running comparison of your stated objectives and your actual results. Remember, without objectives you will not have a basis for corrective action. Hence, your ability to manage your firm will be lessened significantly.

Understanding Printouts and Forms

Successful simulation play requires understanding printouts and forms. There are several forms and sample printouts that you must understand thoroughly in order to play **Marketing Simulation** effectively. These forms have been provided to simplify your decision-making processes. The following paragraphs present a brief introductory explanation of these forms. You should read this section carefully and familiarize yourself with these forms because you will be referring to them regularly as you read the remainder of this book.

The following is a list of the printouts and forms and their locations:

1. Objectives and Planning Form, Form 1 (see Appendix C)
2. Model Description Chart (see Table 3.2)
3. Marketing Research Request Form, Form 2 (see Chapter 1, the DSS disk, and Appendix C)
4. Marketing Research Results (see Chapter 4)
5. Management Decision Form, Form 3 (see Chapter 1, the DSS disk, and Appendix C)
6. Income Statement (see Table 2.1 and Appendices A and D)
7. Ratio Analysis (see Chapter 5 and Appendix D)
8. Balance Sheet (see Table 2.2 and Appendix D)
9. Profit Analysis (see Chapter 3 and Appendix D)
10. Inventory Analysis (see Chapter 3, DAT on the DSS disk, and Appendix D)
11. Sales Information (see output on the DSS disk and Appendix D)
12. Profit Planning Form, Form 4 (see DAT on the DSS disk and Appendix C)
13. Research and Development Expenditure Form, Form 5 (see DAT on the DSS disk and Appendix C)
14. Distribution Expense Planning Form, Form 9 (see DAT on the DSS disk and Appendix C)
15. Sources and Uses of Funds Form, Form 6 (see DAT on the DSS disk and Appendix C)

Objectives and Planning Form, Form 1, gives you a format as well as a written record of your objectives, strategies, and tactics. This form is intended mainly for major objectives. However, you should also keep a record of your specific objectives in such areas as sales forecasting and production scheduling, operating expenses, and so forth. Since you will find it beneficial to specify your objectives clearly for each quarter, you should always take time to use this form. Blank Objectives and Planning Forms are located in Appendix C.

Table 3.2 is the **Model Description Chart**. This chart lists all of the 16 different TV models; you may select up to 4 of these models to produce and market. The chart provides information on each model's features and its production cost. Information on how to use this chart is contained in Chapter 3.

The **Marketing Research Request Form**, Form 2, is your mechanism for purchasing marketing research information to aid in your decision making. Detailed instructions on how to complete this form are provided in Appendix B. You may find copies of this form in Appendix C; you will find that you may complete this form on the DSS disk as well.

The marketing research request form is always completed one quarter in advance of when you need the research information. Therefore before you make your first management decision regarding production, pricing, and promotion of TV models you will probably want some marketing research information to help you make this decision—to help you determine the "best" TV models, how many units to produce, and so forth. Consequently the first task in **Marketing Simulation** is to complete the marketing research request form. Your instructor will then provide you with the marketing research information you requested (if any) and you will be prepared to make your first decision for Year 1, Quarter 1 on the Management Decision Form. As you make decisions for Year 1, Quarter 2, you will probably also complete another Marketing Research Request Form so that you will have research information to aid you in making decisions for Year 1, Quarter 2. Remember, you must always buy marketing research in *advance* of the decision period for which you expect to use the information.

When you purchase marketing research information by entering a Y for the appropriate marketing research study on the request form, your information will appear on a printout labeled **Marketing Research Results**. Each marketing research study that is available for you to purchase is explained in Chapter 4. Examples of printouts of these studies are provided in Appendix D.

The **Management Decision Form**, Form 3, is the form on which you will implement your marketing strategy decisions. Basically, you use this form to select which TV models to market as well as their prices, promotion method and expenditures, quantities to be produced, types and numbers of dealers, and the amount you wish to invest in research and development (R & D). Like the Marketing Research Request Form, this form is also on your DSS disk and blank forms are provided in Appendix C. Instructions on using this form are located in Appendix B. Please be extremely careful in completing this form. A careless mistake may cost you thousands of dollars in lost profits. It is strongly recommended that you make copies of your Team DSS disk before you submit it to your instructor so that you will have a record of your decisions.

The **Income Statement** is a standard accounting form that reflects the amount of profits (or losses) a company incurs during a given period. Basically, the income statement specifies the revenues that have been generated from sales minus the expenses incurred to make those sales. The difference is the profit or loss.

The income statement in Table 2.1 is your firm's most recent income statement. It will help you understand how your income statement will be calculated. It is explained in detail in Appendix A. An example of the income statement printout that you will receive is located in Appendix D. New income statements for each quarter will be provided to you on the DSS disk. By accessing the Print Company Reports option on your DSS you will be able to print a hard copy or view your income statement on your computer screen.

The **Ratio Analysis** section is provided to allow you to evaluate the efficiency of your management decisions by the use of standard financial ratios. These ratios are explained in Chapter 5. An example of a ratio analysis section is contained in Appendix D. The ratio analysis for each new quarter of simulation will also be provided to you on the DSS disk by accessing the Print Company Reports option.

The **Balance Sheet** is a standard accounting form that reflects a company's financial position at a given time. Basically, the balance sheet specifies a company's assets and liabilities. The difference is the company's net worth. A copy of your company's most recent balance sheet is shown in Table 2.2. A sample printout of a balance sheet is located in Appendix D. Updated balance sheets will be provided on your DSS disk. You may view or print copies by accessing the Print Company Reports menu option.

At the bottom of your balance sheet printout in Appendix D are two additional sections that you will find very helpful: (1) profit analysis and (2) inventory analysis.

The **Profit Analysis** section is provided to aid you in determining the profits (or losses) you are earning on each TV model you are marketing. This section should be useful in making your marketing decisions and is explained in Chapter 3. An example of a profit analysis section is included in the balance sheet printout in Appendix D and you will find your Profit Analysis for each quarter of the simulation by accessing the Print Company Reports menu option.

The **Inventory Analysis** section is very important in keeping an accurate record of the units of TV sets you have in inventory. This section will provide you with information on the number of units you have in beginning inventories, units produced in overtime, units sold, and the number of units in ending inventories. If you have units left in inventory at the end of the year you sell all of those units to customers in the industrial market at 90 percent of their production cost. These sales, if any, will be reported in the fourth quarter only and will appear as industrial sales in the inventory analysis section. A sample inventory analysis section is provided in the balance sheet printout in Appendix D. Again, you should access the Print Company Reports menu item to observe your inventory analysis.

The **Sales Information** printout contains information that you will receive along with your income statement and balance sheet printouts each quarter. (See Appendix D and your DSS disk.) The sales information printout specifies product sales by submarket and by distribution channel. You are provided with the prices and all product models being marketed by your competitors and the market shares of each model. Market share figures are also provided by type of dealer and for the total submarket.

In the lower section of the sales information printout you will find a record of your cumulative **R & D expenditures** and your **R & D index**. This reports how much you have spent on R & D to date and what effect these expenditures have had on technology. Your DSS disk automatically keeps up with your R & D expenditures and you may observe graphs of these expenditures by accessing the DAT menu option. Or, you may manually keep a record of your quarterly R & D expenditures on Form 5, which is in Appendix C. Also, should you experience an R & D breakthrough, a message informing you of the nature of the breakthrough will appear below your R & D index. R & D is discussed in Chapter 3.

At the bottom of the sales information printout is each company's **earnings per share** (EPS) for the current quarter and for the entire period of the game. EPS is the main yardstick you should use to compare your profit standing with that of your competitors. This information may be graphed using the DAT option on your DSS disk.

The **Profit Planning Form**, Form 4, is provided to help you analyze your planned pricing decision. This form allows you to estimate sales revenue based on your selected prices, costs of sales, operating expenses, and income. This form is explained in the Profit Planning section in Chapter 3, and is contained on the DAT portion of your DSS disk. Additionally a copy of this form is provided in Appendix C.

The **Distribution Expense Planning Form**, Form 9, is located in Appendix C and is in the DAT section of your DSS disk, under Dealer Expenses. As you will learn, you have several alternative distribution strategies: selecting different types of dealers and adding, shifting, or deleting dealers. Expenses are associated with each strategy you implement, and this form is useful in calculating your distribution expenses for each quarter.

The **Sources and Uses of Funds Analysis Form**, Form 6, is provided to help you calculate your cash on hand. You should use this form to determine your cash flow as you operate your company. Sources and uses of funds are explained in Appendix A, and the form may be found in Appendix C. You will also be able to analyze your cash flow projections by using a computerized version of this form, which is contained in the DAT portion of your DSS, under the heading Cash Flow.

You are not expected to understand fully the functions of all of these forms and printouts at this point. However, as these items appear in your reading you may find it helpful to refer back to this section for a brief description and the location of an example. It is hoped that by the time you have completed this book you will understand all of the forms and printouts you will use in **Marketing Simulation**.

At this point you should have a general frame of reference for understanding **Marketing Simulation**. You should now be prepared to learn more about the industry in which you will compete as well as the current financial condition of your firm. You will be introduced to your firm's current balance sheet and most recent income statement in Chapter 2.

HOW TO OPERATE YOUR STUDENT DSS DISK

This section gives you step-by-step instructions on how to start up, move about, and interact with your DSS disk. As we noted earlier, we want you to become familiar with it as soon as possible. You can go ahead and see how it works before your Instructor assigns teams or even talks about **Marketing Simulation** in class.

Throughout our description, we are assuming that you have some limited knowledge of DOS commands. If you do not, or you are unsure, we urge you to confer with your local personal computer consultant about the instructions that are confusing to you.

Preliminaries: Copying BASIC onto Your DSS Disk

First, you must copy the BASIC programming language onto your DSS Disk. We cannot provide it on the disk because it is protected

16 Marketing Simulation

by copyright. Also, there is more than one version of BASIC, and you must use the one that is compatible with your computer.

This is the only step with which you may need some help, and your instructor will probably be able to assist you. Detailed instructions are available in Appendix F.

Getting into the DSS Program

Now, lets assume that you have already copied BASIC onto your DSS disk. To begin the DSS program:

1. Start up your computer with a DOS system disk.
2. You want to get to the A: prompt. Depending on how the DOS system disk is configured, you may have to (one, some, all, or none of the following):
   a. enter in the day (or just press Return)
   b. enter in the time (or just press Return)
   c. exit to DOS
3. Put the DSS Disk in Drive A. You should see the cursor just to the right of the A: prompt.
4. Type in STUDENT and press Return.
5. **Marketing Simulation** will install BASIC, then load and run the simulation.
6. You will see the logo of **Marketing Simulation** and the authors' names on the screen. To move on to the next screen, press any key as noted on the logo screen.

Running DIS

To see how the initial menu for DIS will appear on your screen, see Table 1.3.

TABLE 1.3
MARKETING SIMULATION INITIAL MENU

MARKETING SIMULATION–STUDENT DSS
MANAGEMENT DECISION FORM

1. Industry Set-Up–First Step
2. Management Decision Form
3. Marketing Research Request Form
4. Utility Menu
5. Print Company Reports
6. EXIT to DAT (Decision Analysis Tools)
7. EXIT to DOS
Enter Selection (1-7) and Press <ENTER> :

As you can see, there are seven choices available. Each one is now described.

Industry Set-Up: Allows you to enter in your team's designation (e.g., Industry A, Team 1) and to type in your team members' names.

The Industry Set-Up screen will present you with a blank form on which you can enter team members' names. When you see the

Industry Set-Up screen for the first time, you will see that the company on your DSS Disk is Company X-1. Company X-1 will appear here until your instructor takes your disk and returns it with your assigned industry, company designation. At that time you may enter the names of your team members. Don't forget to press the Return key after entry. Follow the instructions on the bottom of the screen to make entries, corrections, save your input, or exit the screen.

Management Decision Form: Moves you to a screen where you will enter in all of your decisions except marketing research. That is, you will specify the model, price, production, advertising, sales force, and other levels for the coming quarter. You have already seen this form; it is Table 1.1.

The Management Decision Form shown in Table 1.1 corresponds to the last decisions made by the managers of the company you are taking over. Whenever you access it during simulation play, your Industry, Company Number, Year, and Quarter will automatically appear in the proper spots. During actual play, your company's decisions from the previous quarter will be on the form, and you can change them for the current quarter by specifying the location of each decision you want to change. This will cause the cursor to go to that location and allow you to enter in the new numbers. Hitting the Enter key will signal the program that you are finished with that particular change and want to go on to the next one. When you are through with your changes, pressing the Enter key will save them and return you to the initial menu. Typing EX will allow you to exit without saving any changes you have made.

Marketing Research Request Form: Moves you to the Marketing Research Studies menu, from which you can select those you wish to have performed. This is Table 1.2.

The Marketing Research Request Form will also automatically indicate your company designation, year, and quarter. You should note that the management of the company you are taking over did not purchase any marketing research last quarter, as can be seen in Table 1.2. During actual play, your last quarter's marketing research selections will automatically appear. To make a selection from the 12 different marketing research studies, all you need do is to enter in the number and press Enter. When you do this, the Y or N column will change from N to Y, and the charge for the research study will be added to the total. If you decide that you do not want that study after all, repeating the number and pressing the Return key will change it back to N. When you are finished with this form, pressing the Return key will save it and return you to the Initial menu.

Utility Menu: Allows you to set computer disk drives, printer codes, and so forth. You will be accessing a Lotus 1–2–3 or spreadsheet package in order to operate your DAT. Option 1, Student Disk Drive Assignment, allows you to specify into which disk drive you will place your Student DSS disk and into which drive you will place Lotus 1–2–3. If you have a dual disk drive system, you should designate the drives as follows:

1. Drive for Spreadsheet   B
2. Drive for Student DSS disk   A

If you have a hard drive, you should designate the drives as follows:

1. Drive for Spreadsheet   C
2. Drive for Student DSS disk   A

You will also see an option for entering the command that will invoke your Lotus program (this is usually either 123 or LOTUS). (Of course, you must have your spreadsheet program [i.e., Lotus 1–2–3] loaded on your hard drive.)

The Utility Menu also allows you to set some commands for your printer. The printed output requires that you use the compressed print ASCII code.

Print Company Reports: Goes to the routine for printing out all of your company's financial and other performance reports either on the printer attached to your computer or on your computer screen.

Exit to DAT: Moves you to the decision analysis tools aspect of your DSS. See below for detailed instructions.

Exit to DOS: Exits **Marketing Simulation**.

To select any one of these options, all you need to do is type in the number of your choice and press the Return key. The computer will move you to the appropriate screen and instruct you on how to use that routine.

Moving to DAT from DIS

Option 6 will move you into the DAT part of your DSS. You should remember that DAT requires Lotus 1–2–3 or a compatible spreadsheet program in order to run. When you enter 6 and press Enter, you will be instructed to have your DSS disk in a certain disk drive and to have Lotus 1–2–3 in another disk drive. You can change the disk drive configuration, including using a hard drive, by using the Disk Drive Assignments routine in the Utility Menu.

Let's suppose that you have a dual disk drive, and **Marketing Simulation** has been set up for the DSS in Drive A and Lotus 1–2–3 in Drive B. When you select option 6 from the Initial Menu, the program will remind you to place the DSS Disk in Drive A, and then it will remind you to have your Lotus 1–2–3 disk in Drive B. With each reminder, the program will pause, and you will need to hit any key to move it to the next instruction. It will then start up Lotus 1–2–3 with the instruction "123" which is the normal start up command for Lotus 1–2–3. If your Lotus 1–2–3 has been altered to start up with a different command, you will need to specify the command on the disk drive assignment section of the Utility Menu.

Loading DAT Without Using the Student DSS Disk

Because DAT is a stand-alone network of Lotus 1–2–3 templates, you can operate it independently. There are two ways to load it. First, if Lotus 1–2–3 is already loaded and you are looking at the Lotus screen selections menu, put your DSS disk in the Lotus files disk drive and issue the Lotus commands:

/FR (Note: this means "press /, then press F, then press R")

Lotus will then ask you for the file name and display all template files along the top of the blank spreadsheet. Put the cursor over the file name, MASTER, and press Return. The DAT will be loaded.

On the other hand, if Lotus 1−2−3 is not loaded on your computer, load it either from your hard disk or a Lotus 1−2−3 disk. When the computer prompts you to put in Disk B, place your DSS in the disk drive, and the DAT program will automatically load.

Running DAT

Once DAT is loaded by Lotus 1−2−3, you will see the initial screen which holds the Initial Menu. On the very top line, you will see a designation such as "M1: PR [W80]." Ignore this line on all screens.

The cursor will be on the second line, and it can be moved with your left or right cursor movement keys across the words on that line. These words are menu items, and the third line will provide a brief explanation of each choice. As you move the cursor from one menu item to the next, you will see the third line change to coincide with the selection highlighted by the cursor.

The majority of your screen will be taken up with text if you are looking at instructions. It will be taken up with a form if you are looking at one of the planning tools such as the Sources and Uses of Funds form, or it will be a graph if you are looking at one of the graphing procedures.

The Initial DAT Menu contains several informative selection options. They are:

Go	Go to the Master Menu
Explain DAT	Explains what DAT is and how it works
Overview	Overview of what routines are in DAT
Warnings	Notes some errors you might make using DAT
Restarting	Tells you that by pressing ALT and R simultaneously, you can restart DAT from any routine where you may have made an error.
Disk Full	What to do if you save too many graph files and your disk has run out of space
Quit	Leaves Lotus 1−2−3

Whenever you make a selection (except for Quit, of course), you will be moved to a new screen with the menu items listed on the second line and a brief explanation for the highlighted menu item just below it. DAT has been designed to allow you to move throughout it by using the menu selections. Once you have made a selection and that screen has come up, you can move "down" the menu deeper and deeper into that routine by making selections on successive screens, or you can move "up" the menu by selecting the "Previous" or "Return" menu options.

The Master Menu: Accessing the Tools

From the Initial Menu, you can "Go" to the Master DAT Menu. This is the master selection menu for the decision analysis tools we have programmed for you to use in **Marketing Simulation**. There are six options in the Master Menu:

Templates   (Templates are blank forms.)
Moves you to another menu from which you can select the template for the form you desire:
Profit Planning Form
Cash Flow Analysis Form
Dealer Expenses Form

History   Graphical analysis of most of your past decisions, displayed quarter by quarter

Competition   Graphs of the performance of all competitors such as sales, market share, and so forth

Inventory   Graphs of inventory decisions results by product

Forecasting   Sales forecasting techniques applied to your products

Break-even   Perform and graph break-even analysis for various price levels

Using the Tools

Basically, there are two types of tools. First, there are forms such as the Cash Flow analysis, which instructs you to enter the various Sources and Uses of funds for the coming quarter so you can determine whether or not your company will experience a cash shortfall. DAT will give you an option of printing out the completed form and keeping it for later reference.

Second, there are graphs. Graphs afford visual presentation of a large amount of data, and you can study them for trends or valuable patterns that will help you better see your company's operations or perhaps perceive competitive advantages. Lotus 1–2–3 will not allow direct printing of graphs, so the DAT is programmed to let you save the graph as a file for later access and printing by Lotus PrintGraph, if you wish. Be sure to give each graph file a unique name if you save it; otherwise, Lotus 1–2–3 will simply erase the old file and replace it with the new one under the same name.

Practicing with DIS and DAT

Practice entering decisions and grow accustomed to moving around the DIS. You will soon realize that you can change anything very easily. Also, as we have noted earlier, the DSS disk that came with this manual has a practice data set for DAT (for Company X-1), and you are urged to try it out as soon as possible to become comfortable with its menu selections, forms, and wealth of graphs.

Chapter 2
The Industry and Your Company

THE INDUSTRY

The television industry is highly competitive in terms of price, advertising, distribution, and consumers' perceptions of product quality. This marketing simulation has been programmed to closely approximate the TV industry, though modifications have been made to decrease the complexity of your decisions. Bear in mind, however, that you should not use current information about the television industry as a basis for your decisions. The description of the industry provided in this book gives you the basic details needed for success in **Marketing Simulation**.

Your instructor will assign you to an industry and a company. Each industry may consist of up to five companies. It is important to remember that only companies in the same industry actually compete against one another. Your company's decisions will in no way affect another company in another industry, and likewise, decisions of companies in other industries will not affect you. For example, if your company is in Industry A, you will not be affected in any way by companies competing in other industries such as B or C. Therefore you will never have more than four competitors.

YOUR COMPANY

Your Income Statement

Every company begins with identical operating revenues, costs, and profits. A company's financial position is reflected by two standard accounting forms: the balance sheet and the income statement. These are important sources of information, and you should understand them fully before you begin playing **Marketing Simulation**. These two forms will be the basic feedback letting you know how your company performed on the basis of the decisions you made.

22 Marketing Simulation

In the following paragraphs we will introduce you to your company by briefly examining your balance sheet and income statement. Please refer to the income statement and the balance sheet in Tables 2.1 and 2.2 as you read. Because some students may be a bit rusty on basic accounting concepts, you will find a detailed explanation of the income statement in Appendix A.

The former (fictitious) management of your firm made the set of management decisions shown in Table 1.1. These decisions produced the results shown in Tables 2.1 and 2.2 on your beginning income statement and balance sheet.

If you examine the income statement in Table 2.1, you will find that in the last fictitious quarter of operation your firm made a net profit (income after taxes) of $146,855. To generate this profit the firm produced and sold 4,463 units of four different TV sets (you will select new sets from those listed in Table 3.2 for your first decision), for total gross sales of $1,357,760. It cost the firm $800,050 to produce the TV models that were sold. Subtracting cost of sales from gross sales results in gross margin ($1,357,760 − $800,050 = $557,710).

Subtracting operating expenses from gross margin yields income before taxes ($557,710 − $264,000 = $293,710). Taxes are always 50 percent of income before taxes ($293,710 × 0.50 =

TABLE 2.1
YOUR COMPANY'S MOST RECENT INCOME STATEMENT

Sales					
B					$120,450
G					245,860
K					547,200
P					444,250
Gross Sales					$1,357,760
Cost of Sales:	B	G	K	P	
Beginning Inventory	845	0	9,600	57,600	
Current Production	48,100	112,500	270,000	270,000	
Overtime Production	3,575	18,590	9,240	0	
Storage Charge	0	0	0	0	
Available for Sale	52,520	131,090	288,840	327,600	
Ending Inventory	0	0	0	0	
Cost of Sales	52,520	131,090	288,840	327,600	800,050
Gross Margin					557,710
Operating Expenses					
Promotions		80,000			
Dealer Expense		50,000			
Dealer Change Expense		0			
Personal Selling		90,000			
Marketing Research		0			
Research & Development		0			
Model Change Expense		0			
Administration		20,000			
Depreciation		24,000			
Interest Charge		0			264,000
Income Before Taxes					293,710
Income Tax					146,855
Income After Taxes					146,855
Earnings Per Share					1.469

TABLE 2.2
YOUR COMPANY'S BALANCE SHEET

Cash	$ 438,900
Inventory	0
Net Plant & Equipment	1,204,000
Total Assets	$1,642,900
Liabilities and Owner's Equity	
Accounts Payable	$0
Capital Stock ($1 Par Value)	100,000
Retained Earnings	1,542,900
Total Liabilities and Owners Equity	$1,642,900

$146,855). This leaves income after taxes of $146,855 which is divided by the number of outstanding shares of common stock (100,000). This results in earnings per share of $1.469 ($146,855 divided by 100,000 = $1.469). Earnings per share, or EPS, is a yardstick for measuring your firm's quarterly performance against that of competing firms. EPS and a cumulative EPS called "game EPS" are calculated for all firms and reported at the bottom of the sales information printout. Also, financial ratios will be provided for you to help you determine the efficiency of your managerial decisions. This is explained fully for you in Chapter 5.

Your Balance Sheet

The balance sheet is a statement indicating the amount of assets a company possesses and also the amount of its liabilities. Your company will receive a balance sheet similar to the one in Table 2.2 each time you make a decision. (See Appendix D for a computer printout of a balance sheet.)

You may assume that the balance sheet in Table 2.2 is your company's present balance sheet. All companies begin **Marketing Simulation** with identical assets and liabilities. Therefore all competing companies have the same balance sheet.

To better understand your firm's present financial position, examine your balance sheet in more detail. You have a cash balance of $438,900. The first thing you will want to know is, "How much money do I have available to spend?" Understanding sources and uses of funds, also known as cash flow analysis, is helpful in answering this question. This is explained in Appendix A.

It is important to point out that should your uses of cash ever exceed your sources of cash, a bank will lend you what is needed to stay in business. The bank, of course, will charge you interest at the rate of 16 percent per year, or 4 percent per quarter. The amount of the loan will be the amount that will bring your company up to a zero cash position. It will automatically be recorded in the accounts payable account on your balance sheet. The interest on the loan will be recorded the following quarter in the interest charge account on the income statement.

You will also note that you do not have any inventory. This means that you completely sold out all units in inventory during your "last" (fictitious) operating period; this left a $0 inventory valuation on your balance sheet.

Net plant and equipment is valued at $1,204,000 and will decrease each quarter by a fixed amount of depreciation—$24,000. This will appear each quarter as an operating expense on your income statement.

You do not owe any money at present, so your accounts payable account is $0. Your firm has 100,000 shares of outstanding stock valued at $1 par. Therefore, the capital stock account is $100,000 and will remain so for the entire simulation.

The retained earnings account will increase by the amount of income after taxes each quarter or, of course, decrease by the amount of losses should they be incurred. Since retained earnings is a cumulative account, it is a good yardstick for measuring your company's progress over time. Your company currently has $1,542,900 in retained earnings. You should strive to increase this figure by earning profits during the simulation.

The preceding discussion has introduced you to statements of your financial position. As mentioned previously, a section of Appendix A is devoted to an explanation of the income statement. This section will aid you in your understanding of each entry on your income statement. It is important that you understand this form fully when playing **Marketing Simulation**. The following chapters introduce you to the elements of marketing strategy—market segmentation and the marketing mix variables (product, distribution channels, pricing, and promotion). Each chapter begins with a brief introduction, followed by a discussion of how you may implement your company's marketing strategy.

Chapter 3
Marketing Strategy

THE MEANING OF MARKETING STRATEGY

While objectives establish the results you are trying to achieve, **marketing strategy** outlines the actions necessary to achieve those objectives. A marketing strategy consists of two interrelated elements: (1) the selection of a market or market segment as the firm's **target market**, which is the market to which a company wishes to appeal, and (2) the selection of a **marketing mix** to be used in appealing to this target market. A firm's marketing mix is the way it implements the controllable marketing variables. Broadly speaking, the controllable marketing variables may be classified into the following four categories: (1) product, (2) price, (3) distribution channel, and (4) promotion. However, each of these categories represents many different variables. (See Table 3.1.)

A marketing strategy may be thought of as an overall plan for accomplishing objectives. As an example, consider the following elements of a possible marketing strategy:

1. Selecting a specific target market
2. Developing the highest-quality product possible
3. Charging a premium price
4. Promoting more heavily than competitors
5. Distributing the products only through specialty stores

An alternate strategy might be

1. Selecting another target market
2. Developing an average-quality product
3. Charging a low price
4. Spending the same amount on promotion as competitors
5. Distributing the product through discount houses, supermarkets, and drugstores

A marketing strategy must include decisions regarding each of the four marketing mix categories—product, price, distribution, and

TABLE 3.1
ADDITIONAL MARKETING MIX VARIABLES

Product Variables	Price Variables	Distribution Variables	Promotion Variables
Quality	Basic Price	Distribution Channels	Advertising
Style	Credit Terms	Outlet Locations	Personal Selling
Features	Discounts & Allowances	Inventory	Sales Promotions
Service		Transportation	Publicity
Warranty		Dealer Coverage	
Brand Name			
Options			
Product Line			
Patents			

promotion. **Product strategy** refers to plans involving product variables—quality, style, brand name, packaging, and so forth—that are undertaken to achieve company objectives. **Price strategy** refers to plans involving the price variables—basic price points, credit terms, discounts, and so forth—that are undertaken to achieve company objectives. **Distribution strategy** refers to plans involving the distribution variables, and **promotion strategy** refers to plans involving the promotion variables. Each of these areas of marketing strategy is discussed in later sections of this chapter.

Marketing strategy and marketing tactics are often confused. A **tactic** is a specific change that you make in carrying out your strategy. Assume that you have decided on a strategy of pricing your products very low. Changing your price from $9.95 to $9.27 would be a tactic—a specific move guided by your overall strategy. You will set overall plans—strategies—for each of your marketing variables. Your tactics will be specific adjustments in those variables for the purpose of carrying out your strategy.

DETERMINING YOUR COMPANY'S MARKETING STRATEGY

There are many strategies, or "plans of action," that may enable you to compete successfully in **Marketing Simulation**. However, you should keep in mind the fact that your assumptions on which those strategies are based may prove to be incorrect, and you should not hesitate to change your strategy decisions. As a matter of fact, in industry it often happens that when one firm is very successful, rival firms initiate similar strategies, thereby forcing the original firm to change its strategy. Therefore, you must not only implement strategy but also continuously monitor market changes and make strategy alterations in anticipation of competitive changes. The decision analysis tools (DAT) provided in **Marketing Simulation** will prove invaluable to you in monitoring the market and your competition.

Of the many strategies available to you, you may adopt, for example, a strategy of penetration pricing—or pricing your television sets relatively low in an attempt to gain a large share of industry sales. This "discount pricing" strategy may be successful, but you must keep in mind the fact that a competitor may reduce the effectiveness of your price by having a much larger network of dealers or spending more on promotion. Also, remember that you want to "mix" marketing variables properly. For example, the price advantage that you may obtain by having a lower price would be facilitated even further by a promotional program that communicates the availability of your product at your competitive price to the consumers in your target market.

Determining your firm's marketing strategy involves selecting your target market and setting a plan for each of the marketing variables. For example, you will make strategy decisions regarding the market segment or segments you wish to attract, types of TV sets you will produce, their prices, your distribution channels, and the amount to be spent on the various forms of promotion. These decisions, taken together, represent your company's "marketing mix." Your company should strive to develop a competitive marketing mix that meets the needs and wants of the customers in your target market.

Though your competitors will be marketing essentially the same product as your company—TV sets—the diversity of marketing variables allows you to implement many different strategy alternatives. For example, consider two successful competing firms that produce essentially the same products but have a different marketing mix. Revlon and Avon are both marketers of cosmetics. They produce essentially the same products at comparable prices, but here the similarities end. The two companies promote and distribute their cosmetics completely differently. Revlon's strategy involves the use of large, eye-catching, attractive displays in department and variety stores. Avon's strategy depends almost exclusively on the use of salespeople to promote and distribute its cosmetics door to door.

MARKET SEGMENTATION

A **market** may be defined as people with the willingness to buy and the ability to buy. Markets for goods and services are not usually viewed as homogeneous entities whose members have the same needs, wants, income, educational level, and so forth. It is more realistic to view the marketplace as an aggregate of groups of people with different needs and wants. These groups are referred to as **submarkets** or **market segments**. The practice of viewing the market as several different segments of consumers with various needs, incomes, and so forth, is referred to as **market segmentation**.

Any discussion of marketing strategy should consider market segmentation. The market for automobiles, for example, may be thought of as several different market segments. There is a segment that desires an expensive, luxurious car; a separate segment desires an economical, thrifty car as a cheap means of transportation; and so on. Volkswagen's marketing strategy involves a marketing mix that appeals to a particular market segment, whereas Lincoln's marketing strategy involves a different marketing mix for a different market segment.

A firm may have different product strategies tailored to different market segments. IBM, for example, produces different models of computers designed to meet the unique requirements of various market segments. These segments vary substantially in computing ability, features desired, and willingness to pay high prices for a computer. Careful consideration of these market segments is the basis of a substantial component of IBM's marketing strategy.

Market segmentation has become a widely used marketing practice. A company that engages in market segmentation may offer individual consumers a product that is better tailored to their specific needs than a company that views the marketplace as one large group of undifferentiated potential consumers—a practice referred to as **undifferentiated marketing**. To see why, imagine a firm that markets one type of shampoo. This firm views the market as an undifferentiated group of consumers. It assumes that this one type of shampoo, its price, its distribution, and its promotion appeal to the total market. Therefore the total market—all consumers—is the firm's target market. Now imagine another shampoo firm that practices market segmentation. Breck, for instance, markets different shampoo products to fit the needs of consumer groups with different hair "problems" ("too dry," "too oily," etc.). A consumer who has one of these hair problems is likely to purchase the shampoo designed "especially" for him or her—the one that satisfies the specific needs of consumers in that particular market segment—instead of the shampoo produced for "everyone." Consequently the firm engaging in market segmentation gains a sale at the expense of the company practicing undifferentiated marketing.

The preceding discussion points out the positive side of market segmentation. The negative side of market segmentation is that it is expensive. Developing several different products, prices, distribution channels, and promotion techniques is more costly than having a single production run, price, and method of distribution and promotion. Therefore marketing decision makers must weigh the sales to be made from market segmentation against the costs of implementing such a strategy.

Market Segmentation in Marketing Simulation

In **Marketing Simulation** you may view the total television market as consisting of four submarkets. You should consider several factors in selecting your submarket or submarkets. How many potential sales does the submarket represent? How many competitors are likely to be attracted to that submarket? What profits do you anticipate from marketing your TV sets in only one submarket, in two submarkets, in three submarkets, or all four submarkets?

The consumers represented in the four submarkets need different-sized TV sets and different features on the sets as well as different prices. A general description of each of the four submarkets is provided here. You may assume that these general attributes are relatively stable and will not vary during the simulation play.

Submarket 1 represents approximately 18 percent of total industry unit sales. This submarket's consumers need black-and-white TV sets of various sizes. The most prevalent uses of the sets sold to this submarket are as a second, or perhaps a third, set for the children in the household, to have a totally portable set to take to ball games and other events, and for use in recreational vehicles such as campers and boats. The model description chart in Table 3.2 shows that models A, B, C, and D are configured to appeal to members of this submarket. These models have relatively small screens and have relatively few extra features. They also tend to have low production costs relative to the other models. **Submarket 2** is composed primarily of consumers who desire portable color sets. The sets in this submarket are purchased primarily as second and third sets by middle- to upper-income families. Sales of the sets in submarket 2 represent approximately 29 percent of total industry unit sales. Models E, F, G, and H are designed to appeal to this segment.

Consumers in **submarket 3** are primarily interested in nonportable color television sets. The sets in this market are purchased most often as the primary set in middle income families that desire a wide range of features. Sales to this submarket represent 43 percent of total industry unit sales. Models J, K, L, and M appeal to this submarket.

Submarket 4 represents only 10 percent of total industry unit sales. Consumers in this submarket are generally upper income consumers who desire unique television features such as large screens, stereo sound, and so on. Some of these consumers desire a TV that is more than just a TV. They are interested in peripheral equipment, such as built-in VCRs, a "surround" sound system that emulates the sound as one would hear it in a movie theatre. In other words, these consumers are interested in having a "movie nook" in their homes complete with large, high-resolution screens, VCRs, and a high-tech sound system. Models N, P, R, and S are designed with this submarket in mind.

In the next section you will learn that you "select" your submarkets by producing the TV models that are designed to appeal to those submarkets. Therefore, you make your market segmentation decision by your choice of TV models. You can assume that the model you select to produce and market will sell only in its designated submarket. When you receive your sales information printout and your updated DSS disk from your instructor you will be able to analyze how well you performed in the market segment you targeted.

PRODUCT STRATEGY

In developing a marketing mix a company would be wise to begin by considering the product variable. The choice of product affects all the other marketing variables greatly. The product variable involves a number of questions: What product (or service) will best appeal to the target market? What style? Which features? Can it be patented? What should its brand name be? Should we offer complementary products? (Refer to Table 3.1 for an elaboration of the elements that may be considered in product strategy.) Though many areas of product strategy may be considered by marketing decision makers, the following paragraphs are limited to a discussion of some basic elements of product strategy.

Marketers have learned that they must continually invest in research and development to produce new and innovative products. Today's breadwinners will undoubtedly lose sales in the future. This is because products, like people, have life cycles. They are born, grow (in sales volume), mature (i.e., sales volume levels off) and die (i.e., sales volume declines). Firms must be prepared to introduce new products into the marketplace as existing products fall prey to products introduced by competitors, changing consumer desires, or even government regulations. Continual innovation is required to avoid product obsolescence.

Marketers should also monitor the consumer to determine which styles and features will be demanded in the products of the future. Consumers' preferences change, thus creating new market segments. Existing products may require modification so that they can satisfy the new preferences. For example, as consumers have become better educated and more affluent there has been an increase in the demand for complex, sophisticated cameras. At the same time, however, another growing market segment demands quality photographs from very simple, easy-to-operate cameras in which everything but the shutter release is automatic. These segments have dictated the marketing of two classes of cameras with completely different functions, styles, and features.

Firms should periodically review their products to determine whether those products are profitable. If not, perhaps they should be eliminated. This, however, is not such an easy decision. Firms may continue to market marginal products because they want to avoid problems associated with product elimination. Workers will probably be laid off; existing customers and dealers will be upset. Or the company may want to have the reputation of a "full-line" company. Usually a firm's decision to eliminate a product is determined by an assessment of what the elimination will do to sales of other products that the firm is marketing.

There are many other areas of product strategy with which marketing students should be familiar. The "right" product packaging, labeling, branding, trademarks, patents, and so forth are also important considerations in marketing a product. These topics are usually discussed in marketing textbooks. However, before competing in **Marketing Simulation** you should read the following paragraphs carefully.

Product Strategy in Marketing Simulation

Selecting Your TV Models. As a manufacturer of television sets you will have a choice as to what TV models you want to manufacture. As discussed previously, the total market for television sets may be divided into four submarkets. Generally speaking, certain TV models appeal to one submarket more than another. The major product characteristics that differentiate the submarkets are (1) black-and-white versus color, (2) screen size, (3) extra features, and (4) cost. The Model Description Chart (Table 3.2) shows which TV model options are available. Study this table and decide which model or models your company should market. (You actually "select" your models by filling in the appropriate blanks on your Management Decision Form—see your DSS disk and Appendix B.) You may purchase consumer preference studies from a marketing research firm to help you select the "best" TV models to market. These studies are explained in detail in Chapter 4.

Product strategy and market segmentation joined together determine your company's target marketing strategy. For example, you may opt to market models that appeal to only one segment, or you may decide to market more models, each geared to a different segment, or you may concentrate in, say, two segments by your product selections. Your target marketing strategy is a very important decision because model changes are allowed only at the beginning of each year. In other words, once you implement your target marketing strategy, your company will "live" with it for four successive quarters.

When you decide on a particular combination of submarkets, you will want to design a marketing mix that will appeal to this/these segments. You may want to begin by considering which models to produce and market. Basically, you have three alternate methods of determining which models to market. First, you may simply study the Model Description Chart and the descriptions of the four submarkets and make your decision solely on the basis of your judgement. That is, by assessing the needs and sizes of the submarkets and the features and production costs of the models, you select the model that you believe will have the greatest appeal to a particular submarket.

Another way of making the decision is to get a "feel" or "reading" from the consumers in **Marketing Simulation** about which models they prefer. You may purchase this information from a marketing research firm. To fully understand this alternative you should carefully read the Consumer Preference Studies section in Chapter 4.

If you do not want to rely entirely on marketing research information, you may choose the third alternative: using a combination of "executive" judgement and marketing research studies. The point is you must decide how you want to go about making this decision. Welcome to the world of business decision making!

There is no "secret" method of making this decision. Teams have been successful with all three alternatives. However, this is an important decision and deserves careful consideration. Once you have selected a model to market, you must market that model for a minimum of one year. You can change models at the beginning of each year (Quarter 1), but you will be charged $100,000 for each model you change after the first year of simulation.

Product Features. The Model Description Chart (Table 3.2) shows the TV model options that are available. Examine each model (A through S) and select the ones you want to produce and market. The models vary according to certain basic features. For example, the screen size ranges from 1.5 inches to 50 inches. As a general rule, consumers prefer larger screens to smaller screens. However, you must be careful in using this generalization in making your selections. In certain submarkets there may be large groups of people who desire a small screen to suit a particular need such as portability or the desire for a second or possibly a third set in the home.

All the television models are solid state and include a VHF/UHF channel dial and a VHF/UHF antenna and operate on alternating electrical current (AC). Other features for each model are listed in the column labeled Extra Features in Table 3.2. These extra features are discussed in the following paragraphs.

An extra feature that is available on certain models is automatic fine tuning (AFT). This feature is available only on color television sets because it serves the function of automatically adjusting the set to maintain constant color reception as the channels are changed.

Remote control is another feature provided on certain models. "Remote control" simply means that the viewer may control the operation of the set by means of a hand-held device some distance from the set itself. This gives viewers the convenience of changing the channel or the volume and making other adjustments without moving from their viewing position.

Pushbutton channel selection through a "digital" keyboard is another feature that is available on several models. Pushbutton channel selection operates very much like a hand-held calculator or a touch-tone telephone. That is, a small display panel on the side of the television set contains ten pushbuttons labeled 0 to 9. The viewer selects the channel by punching the channel number on this display panel, and the set immediately adjusts to the desired channel. This feature enables consumers to tune from one channel to another without going through any of those in between.

Some models have an extra feature that allows them to operate on either alternating current (AC) or direct current (DC). This feature is important because it permits complete portability. For example, if a set has this feature a battery may be used to operate the set on direct current. The battery is built into the set and automatically charges as the set works on alternating current. This feature allows the viewer to take the set to a place where there is no electrical outlet, such as the beach.

TV manufacturers have devoted some effort to improving the audio quality. A stereo sound system is available as a special feature on certain models in **Marketing Simulation**. This system greatly enhances the sound quality in these models with two acoustically matched and balanced speakers including 8" woofers and 2-1/4" tweeters. Also included are an amplifier and separate bass and treble controls.

Another feature that is available with the big screen models only is "surround" sound, a high-tech sound system that not only is stereophonic but involves the installation of as many as five speakers in the TV viewing room. The system is designed to recreate the atmospherics in a movie theatre. Coupled with a big screen TV, the sound system allows the viewer/listener to "feel" the rumble of helicopters, passing jets, and so on.

Some models have remote controlled programming. This allows a viewer, using remote control, to preprogram the set to turn on and off automatically, adjust color, contrast, brightness, and so on.

Picture in a Picture (PIP) is a feature available on some models that allows the set to display several pictures from different channels at the same time. This may be an important feature for a consumer wanting to monitor more than one channel at once.

An additional product feature that may vary from one model to another is cabinet construction. There are three different types of cabinets, and each type has both advantages and disadvantages. The model may have a basic molded-plastic cabinet. This type of cabinet has the advantage of being less expensive but it serves only to house and protect the internal components of the television set; it does not add any aesthetic value to the set. This disadvantage may be overcome by the second type of cabinet, a simulated-wood plastic cabinet. These cabinets, even though they are made of plastic, closely resemble wooden cabinets. However, simulated-wood plastic cabinets are more expensive than molded-plastic cabinets, and some consumers simply do not like them. They prefer the third op-

TABLE 3.2
MODEL DESCRIPTION CHART

Model Code	Submarket	Screen Size	Extra Features	Cabinet Construction	Cost of Production
A	1	1.5"	4	1	$ 60
B	1	3"	4	2	$ 65
C	1	5"	4,2,3	1	$ 80
D	1	15"	2,3,4,7	2	$ 90
E	2	5"	4	1	$ 90
F	2	9"	1	2	$ 100
G	2	12"	1,2,3	1	$ 100
H	2	15"	1,2,3,7	2	$ 150
J	3	19"	1,2	2	$ 125
K	3	19"	1,2,3	2	$ 150
L	3	25"	1,2,3	2	$ 175
M	3	26"	1,2,3,7	3	$ 200
N	4	19"	1,2,3,5,7	2	$ 400
P	4	26"	1,2,3,5,7	2	$ 600
R	4	50"	1,2,3,5,6,7,8	2	$1000
S	4	50"	1,2,3,5,6,7,8	3	$1000

KEY
Submarket: 1 = black-and-white screen; 2 = color portables; 3 = color, nonportable; 4 = color with special features
Features: 1 = AFT (automatic fine tuner); 2 = remote control; 3 = pushbutton channel selection; 4 = AC-DC (battery); 5 = stereo sound system; 6 = surround sound; 7 = remote control programming; and 8 = PIP (picture in a picture)
Cabinet construction: 1 = molded plastic; 2 = simulated-wood plastic; 3 = hand-rubbed wood

tion in cabinet construction, a hand-rubbed hardwood cabinet. This type of cabinet is very expensive and is made primarily for market segments that desire a television set not only to provide entertainment but also to serve as a piece of furniture.

You may be wondering why other features have not been listed. Recall that you have the ability to invest dollars in R & D. Should you or your competitors have technological breakthroughs you will be seeing some new features in the market. High definition TV (HDTV), for example, is not yet available in the real world but was discovered through Japanese R & D efforts. HDTV, when available, will bring about TV pictures with the same clarity as a high quality photograph—near-perfect images. You will want to monitor your R & D message center for just such breakthroughs in your industry. R & D messages will appear just below your R & D index on your sales information printout should you experience a technological breakthrough. Table 3.2 lists the cost of production for each model.

Sales Forecasting and Production Scheduling. As a marketing executive you have the responsibility of sales forecasting—estimating how many TV sets your company will sell. You are also responsible for translating this demand forecast into a production schedule—communicating to your "production department" the exact quantities of each model you want produced each quarter.

Sales forecasting is very important to the efficient operation of any company. Firms allocate vast amounts to obtain accurate sales forecasts because forecasting and producing the exact quantities sold avoids certain types of costs. If a company forecasts that sales will be lower than they actually are, this manufacturer and its dealers will experience "stockouts." Customers will be dissatisfied and may switch to another available brand. Dealers will be dissatisfied because they will probably lose sales to competitors. If it can, a company should try to avoid stockout costs by increasing workload schedules, employee hours, and so forth. This, however, results in another cost: overtime. Labor unions normally require a premium pay scale if workers work more than a standard work week. Should a company forecast *more* sales than are actually made, units are left in ending inventories and must be stored. Providing proper storage space, security, insurance, and so forth for those units results in storage costs.

Companies use several different methods to forecast sales. Some companies buy forecasts of their industry's sales from marketing research firms. Other firms use their past sales records to estimate future sales. Still other firms use sophisticated quantitative models that may consider the effect of dozens of variables on future demand. Rarely, however, will a company forecast exactly the number of units demanded. Even large corporations using the most sophisticated sales forecasting techniques sometimes seriously over- or underestimate demand. Companies strive to make a minimum of errors in estimating sales. A "good" sales forecast is one that results in low overtime or storage costs. You should strive to minimize these two costs while playing **Marketing Simulation**.

It is very important that companies in **Marketing Simulation** produce the correct number of units of a product. The "correct" number is one that is close to the number of units demanded by consumers. Because marketing managers change the variables (price, promotion, etc.) that influence demand, marketers must interface with production managers to help determine the quantities of various products to be produced. Accurate sales forecasting and production planning help minimize the problems of over- or underproducing.

Your basic sales forecasting problem in **Marketing Simulation** is to determine how many units of each model your company will sell each quarter. Then you schedule production so that you have *available for sale* the quantity of sets that you expect to sell. Basically, sales forecasting involves examining what has been sold in the past (if available) and adjusting that figure for anticipated changes in the future. You do have some sales data available to you in the first eight quarters of "practice" data available in your Company X-1 DSS data base. Sales, in dollars, is also shown on your most recent income statement in Chapter 2. This information will at least give you some idea of the general level of sales volume that you may expect in the future. However, the economic and competitive conditions that existed in the last quarter are likely to change in the future. There is no substitute for experience in sales forecasting. As you make decisions, you will gain the experience necessary to make accurate forecasts.

Essentially, your sales volume will be a function of (1) the general economic conditions; (2) seasonal trends; (3) your marketing mix; (4) your competitor's marketing mixes; and (5) the level of industry marketing effort. General economic and seasonal trends are programmed into the **Marketing Simulation** environment. You should be able to detect the effects of these factors as you observe changes in your sales volume and in the sales forecasts you receive from the marketing research firm should you decide to purchase them. Of course your sales will be affected by your marketing mix as well as those of your competitors. Should you market a highly preferred TV model, with a lower price, effectively promoted, and distributed through more dealers than your competition, you will probably have a sales volume larger than that of any of your competitors. Finally, the level of total industry marketing "effort" will affect sales volume. "Effort" refers to the level of (1) products available, (2) prices, (3) promotion, and (4) distribution. If all competitors in an industry increase their promotion, then the total industry marketing effort has been increased and industry sales will increase. Likewise, if competitors in an industry lower their levels of marketing effort (lower production, promotion, distribution, and raise price) then industry sales volume will decrease. Of course, varying industry sales will affect your sales volume. All of these factors will affect your sales volume. And, while this makes your sales forecasting decision more complex, these variables are included in **Marketing Simulation** because they exist in the real world. Sales forecasting in the real world is complex.

Sales Forecasting Methods. In **Marketing Simulation**, you have two different methods of sales forecasting available for your use.

Buying a Sales Forecast. First, to aid with the complex task of sales forecasting you may purchase a quarterly sales forecast for each submarket from a marketing research firm. This forecast considers past sales by the industry as a whole, past industry marketing effort, as well as the present business and economic environment. The forecast, which is a fairly accurate estimate of the industry's actual sales, costs $20,000. Because you will want this information before you decide how to schedule production of your TV models, you must purchase this sales forecast one quarter in advance of the time that you make your decisions. Details of this sales forecast are contained in the Quarterly Sales Forecasts section in Chapter 4.

You should keep in mind the fact that the quarterly sales forecast should be used as a rough starting point for making your own sales forecasting and production scheduling decisions. The quarterly sales forecast is an industry forecast, and because you must make a production decision for your company, you must adjust the quarterly sales forecast downward. The unknown element in this decision is not knowing how much to adjust the quarterly sales forecast. One method you may use to help you make this decision is to multiply the quarterly sales forecast by your company's total market share. **Market share** is defined as company sales divided by industry sales and is the percentage of industry sales made by a specific company. Market share percentages will be available on your sales information printout. Your instructor will tell you how many firms are in your industry. Each firm will have an equal market share (i.e., 50 percent, 33.3 percent, 25 percent, or 20 percent) depending on the number of firms.

Note that market share is only the percentage of total industry sales that you made during the *last* quarter. Since you are estimating sales for the future, you should try to make some subjective decisions concerning your future market share. For example, if you think your price will be significantly lower than in the past, you should anticipate a larger market share. If you are cutting back on promotion expenditures, you should anticipate a smaller market share.

Forecasting Based on Historical Pattern. Another forecasting method is to examine your past company sales for a growth pattern. Suppose you plotted sales for your television models across all past quarters of simulation play, and it looked like the graph in Figure 3.1. As you can see, the sales pattern is "bumpy"; that is, it jumps up and down from quarter to quarter for each product. However, you can see a general pattern of steady growth, and if you were to forecast the sales for Year 2, Quarter 1 (the next quarter), you might try to draw a straight line between all the points and approximate where the growth pattern would fall. This is the basic logic of sales forecasting: trying to identify an underlying trend and projecting it to the next quarter. (This would be a good time to experiment with your DAT. Insert your Student DSS disk and select the DAT menu item. The prompts will notify you of your disk drive assignments. Press any key. Once Lotus 1–2–3 is loaded and you folow any prompt you see, the DAT screen appears with Go highlighted on the command line. Press Enter to take you to the main menu of the DAT program. At the command line on the next screen, use the cursor key to move to History. We are going to examine Company X-1's sales history. Press Enter and wait for Lotus to access all the history files. Start will be highlighted; press Enter. At the next command line shown move the highlight over to Sales and press Enter. At Unit Sales press Enter once again and shortly you will see a graph of unit sales plotted over eight quarters for all four models. This graph is similar to Figure 3.1, and you should use this graphical analysis to aid you in your decision making. Of course once you begin your own simulation, your firm's data will appear here instead of the fictitious Company X-1 data. Continue to experiment with some of the other menu items. Are you beginning to see the power of the information that a decision support system may provide for a manager?)

If you wanted to go a bit further, you might to do some computations and try to determine the average percent change across all relevant quarters. But what are the relevant quarters? Generally, the recent past is a better indicator of the near future than the ancient past, so you might only consider the past three quarters. In Figure 3.1, look at Model 4 and notice how quarters 1-2 seem to have a different pattern of growth than quarters 3-4. Most probably the economic and competitive conditions pertaining to quarters 3-4 are more likely to prevail in coming quarter 5 than are those conditions in quarters 1-2. So the average percent change based on the last three quarters is more accurate, and you would simply multiply the sales level for quarter 4 by that percent growth factor to obtain your forecast of your model's sales for the next quarter.

A slightly different method of sales forecasting is **Exponential Smoothing.** In the average percent growth method just described,

SALES IN UNITS

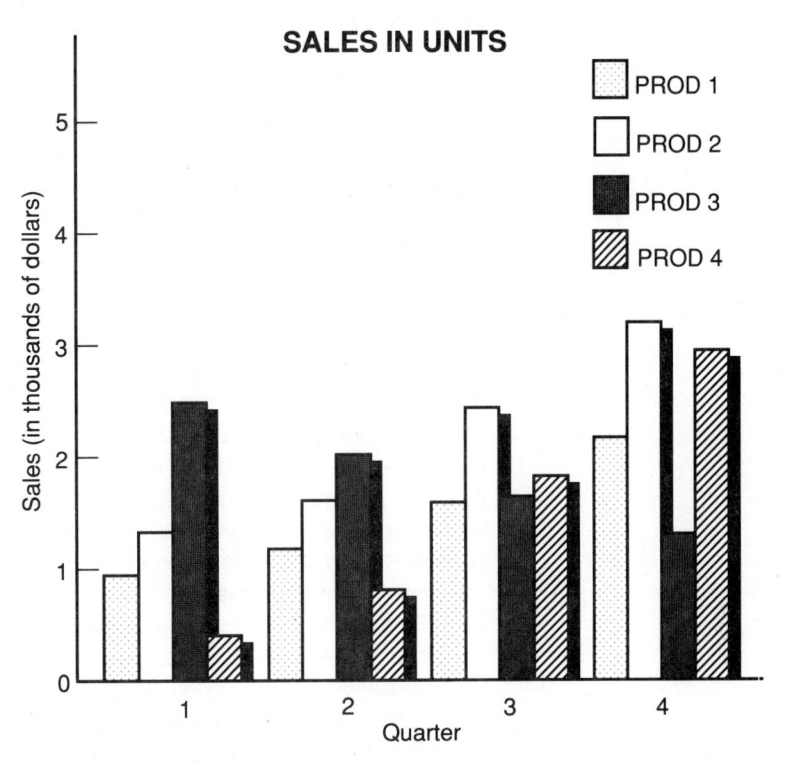

**FIGURE 3.1
GRAPH OF YOUR COMPANY'S SALES**

each of the last three quarters percent change accounted for one-third, but in exponential smoothing, you can weight the last quarter more heavily than the other two quarters. What you are saying when you use exponential smoothing is that the last quarter is more indicative of the conditions in the coming quarter than the previous two quarters. Perhaps you have noticed competitors changing their strategies in the last quarter, or you may have made significant changes in your own marketing strategy last quarter, and you want to take these into account in your sales forecast.

How much more weight should you put on the last quarter if you want to use exponential smoothing? Here are some rules of thumb to keep in mind. If something very significant happened last quarter, and if last quarter's sales differed substantially from the previous two quarters, give it much more weight, say 75 percent; weight the other two at 25 percent. On the other hand, if last quarter's sales reflect a less radical difference, give it about 50 percent weight and let the previous two quarters account for the other 50 percent. If all three quarters seem to reflect the same growth pattern, fall back on the average percent growth forecast method by which each accounts for 33 percent.

Another means of deciding on your sales forecast method is to compare how well the various methods have performed in the past. Selecting the one that best tracks most of your past quarters' sales is often a safe means of deciding. By accessing the DAT of your DSS you will be able to try all three methods of sales forecasting and to see how each performs on your past quarter sales. Unfortunately, sales forecasting is not an exact science, and you should experiment with the different methods for each of the models you are selling. After selecting the Go option, select Forecasting on your next screen's command line. The next screen explains the three forecasting methods; select Start and the Model 1. You may now select any one of the three forecasting techniques described. By selecting a technique you will see a graph that gives you a forecast for the upcoming quarter.

Production Capabilities and Constraints. Once you are satisfied with your sales forecast, you should plan a production schedule for each of your TV models. However, there are a few things you should learn about your company's production capabilities and constraints. First, your company has unionized employees, and your union contract requires that you produce a minimum of 2000 TV sets (total of all models) per quarter. Also since these workers have specialized skills and cannot easily be moved from one type of production to another, your company can change models *only at the beginning of a year.* In any given year, however, you may produce up to four different models. (If you plan to produce fewer than four models, you should consider the effects of the allocation of fixed expense items! See the Profit Planning section.) You may produce all four models in one submarket, one model for each of the four submarkets, or any other combination you desire. The cost of changing models, however, is $100,000 per model changed. This is amortized over a year at $25,000 per quarter and is entered in the model change expense account on the income statement.

Inventory Planning. Regardless of the models you decide to produce, it is very important that you schedule production of each model properly. Ideally, you should have the exact number of models available for sale that you actually sell. However, as mentioned previously, this goal is highly improbable. Companies typically produce either too much or too little. This is also true in **Marketing Simulation.** Should your company produce more than it sells, there will be an ending inventory that must be stored at 5 percent of the production cost of the model. Should your company produce less than is demanded, there will be an overtime charge amounting to 10 percent of the production cost of the model. Production costs for each model are listed in the Model Description Chart (Table 3.2). Of course, like many variables in this simulation, your instructor may elect to change the production costs of these sets. If so, he or she will notify you of the change.

Your company has agreed to sell all TV sets left in inventory at the end of the year to various customers in the industrial market. (The term **industrial market** refers to purchasers who buy products for resale or to be used in the production of other goods or services. The **consumer market** is composed of consumers who buy for personal or family consumption.) Hospitals, retirement homes, hotels, motels, and other companies in the industrial market will always purchase all of your ending inventory at the end of each year at 90 percent of production costs. You have agreed to these terms as a means of clearing your inventory in preparation for a new model year.

You should schedule your production so that *the quantity of models available for sale is equal to the quantity of the sales forecast.* (The phrase Sales Forecast is not shown on the sample inventory analysis below. This is because you should use your sales forecast to determine the number of units available for sale. Available for Sale is shown on the sample inventory analysis.) The quantity available for sale is equal to the quantity of units in beginning inventory *plus* the quantity of units you have in current production. For example, assume that you forecast sales for one of your models to be 6000 units and you have 2000 units of this particular model left in inventory from the previous quarter. (Of course in your first quarter of operation you will not have any units in inventory.) To determine how many units you should produce, you subtract your beginning inventory from your sales forecast. The remainder, 4000, is the quantity you want to produce:

```
  Units forecast to sell          6000
- Units in beginning inventory    2000
= Units to be produced            4000
```

To help you assess your forecasting and inventory planning decisions, you will be provided with an inventory analysis on the lower section of your Balance Sheet Printout each time you make a decision. The inventory analysis section will always be reported in terms of *units* of TV sets—not their dollar value. This analysis will be very important in scheduling production accurately. It will appear in the form depicted in Table 3.3.

TABLE 3.3
SAMPLE INVENTORY ANALYSIS

	Model			
	B	H	M	R
Beginning Inventory	0	500	200	0
Current Production	1500	1600	1500	1200
Overtime Production	0	0	200	420
Available for Sale	1500	2100	1900	1620
Less Sales	1500	2000	1900	1620
Ending Inventory	0	100	0	0

The inventory analysis provides you with the units in beginning inventory for each model, the units in current production plus any overtime production due to excess sales, and a statement of units available for sale from which sales are subtracted. If there is a remainder, this figure is your ending inventory for the present quarter. (Of course ending inventory becomes your beginning inventory for the *next* quarter.)

In Table 3.3 model B had no beginning inventory. The sales forecast for model B was 1500 units, so the number available for sale should be 1500. Remember, you want to have available for sale the *same quantity* as your sales forecast. Since sales forecast − beginning inventory = current production, we determine that current production was 1500 (1500 − 0 = 1500). In this example we see that

40 Marketing Simulation

exactly 1500 units of model B were sold, leaving an ending inventory of 0.

If we examine model H, we find that 500 units were left in beginning inventory from a previous fictitious quarter. The sales forecast was 2100 units. Therefore the decision maker desired to have 2100 units available for sale. Sales forecast (2100) − beginning inventory (500) = current production (1600). In this example, however, actual sales were less than forecast sales, so there was an ending inventory of 100 units of model H. This would become beginning inventory if we were planning a production schedule for model H for another quarter.

Model M had a sales forecast of 1700. (A sales forecast figure may be calculated by adding beginning inventory to current production.) In this example, however, actual sales were greater than forecast sales—1900 units instead of 1700. When this occurs your company *automatically* produces enough units to meet demand by incurring overtime production. Overtime production will always be calculated as the number of units required to equate the quantity available for sale with actual sales. In this case overtime production provides 200 additional units of model M. There is no ending inventory when overtime production is incurred.

For those of you who think you need some practice on inventory calculations, you should examine the inventory analysis for model R and calculate the following[*]:

Beginning inventory = ____

Sales forecast = ____

Current production = ____

Overtime production = ____

Available for sale = ____

Sales = ____

Ending inventory = ____

Sales forecasting and production scheduling will be extremely important to your success in **Marketing Simulation**. Make sure you fully understand the examples given in this book. Also look over the sample printouts to familiarize yourself with the location of important information that you will need in order to forecast and produce accurately.

Inventory planning is a skill that managers develop over time. Often it is advantageous to look at your past production scheduling decisions and see how they resulted in ending inventory. You may find that you always stocked out and had to go into more expensive

---

[*]Answers:
Beginning inventory = 0, sales forecast = 1200, current production = 1200, overtime production = 420, available for sale = 1620, sales = 1620, and ending inventory = 0.

overtime production to meet all of your retailers' orders. On the other hand, you might become aware that you often end up with a large ending inventory and incurred storage charges to hold it until orders came in. We have provided a routine in your DAT that lets you see your past record of (1) beginning inventory, (2) scheduled production, (3) actual sales, and (4) ending inventory for each model across all past quarters of simulation play. We urge you to rely on this tool to refine your production scheduling and inventory analysis. After the Go option, select Inventory. After Lotus accesses the inventory files, start the program and select Product 1. The resulting graph depicts the units produced, overtime production, and the amount of ending inventory. This gives you a historical perspective to aid you in evaluating your decisions in this area.

Sales forecasting and production scheduling will be extremely important to your success in **Marketing Simulation**. Make sure you fully understand the examples given in this book. Also look over the sample printouts to familiarize yourself with the location of important information that you will need in order to forecast and produce accurately. Finally, learn how to use the information provided by the DAT programs of your decision support system.

R & D Expenditures

Many companies allocate money to research and development in an attempt to gain a technological advantage over competing firms. Since television companies operate in a highly competitive industry, they spend substantial sums on R & D. The results of these expenditures have allowed the television industry to place TV sets in 96 percent of the homes in the United States, develop near-perfect color transmission and reception in relatively short time, and make hundreds of features available to fit various consumer needs. Several firms now have models that provide "close-up" picture enlargements by remote control; display the time, date, and channel on the screen by remote control; and have "programmable" channel selection. They also market video tape recorders and videodisc machines that permit consumers to record and play back their favorite programs. Many other product developments are about to be introduced.

R & D may be used in **Marketing Simulation** in the following manner. A company may spend large sums of money on R & D and not receive any significant benefits—technological breakthroughs require more than just money! The models you produce have a certain amount of consumer preference relative to other models. (You may find out what these preferences are through marketing research studies.) These preferences are fairly stable, but if you modify a model by adding product features you may increase consumer preference for your model. The only way you can change the degree of consumer preference for your models is to invest in R & D. By spending money on R & D your company may come up with some new innovation that may be turned into some new feature—a new type of screen, controls, audio, or whatever. You may assume that this new feature will increase customer preference for *all* the TV models you produce and market. Therefore the demand for *all* your sets will increase.

Unfortunately (and realistically), we do not know exactly what amount of expenditure is required to change consumer preferences. However, as soon as your scientists make a feasible technological advance you will be notified on your Sales Information printout. This printout will always report your cumulative R & D expenditures and your R & D index. If you spend enough on R & D, you will experience a technological breakthrough. You will know when this occurs because your R & D index will increase. The R & D index is an index number, which is currently 100. If and when you have a technological breakthrough, the R & D index will *increase*. The greater the impact of the technological breakthrough, the greater the increase in your R & D index. As long as your R & D index remains 100 you have not had a technological breakthrough.

R & D information is provided on your printout in the following form (also examine the sample sales information printout in Appendix D):

YOUR CUMULATIVE R & D EXPENDITURES ARE 8500.

YOUR R & D INDEX IS 100.

This increase in consumer preference will apply to *all* the models you produce, even if you change models. Also, R & D expenditures are *cumulative*. If you invest in R & D in the second quarter and do not do so again until the fourth quarter, you do not lose the investment you made in the second quarter. Therefore you should view R & D as a viable method of substantially improving demand for your models, and it *may* be a good idea to allocate money to R & D so that you may reap the benefits of an increase in consumer demand. Appendix C contains a blank R & D expenditure form on which you can maintain accurate records of your R & D expenditures. Or, you may access DAT and examine your history (of past decisions) to view a record of your expenditures. Select R & D within the History command and you will be given a graph depicting quarterly and cumulative R & D expenditures by quarter.

You should keep in mind the fact that if you change consumer preference for the sets you produce, this change is not available to your competitors through marketing research studies. For example, suppose you find that models B, G, L, and P are ranked first, first, second, and second in consumer preference in submarkets 1, 2, 3, and 4, respectively. (This may be determined by purchasing consumer preference studies.) Your company decides to produce these sets and also to spend substantial amounts on R & D. After an unknown length of time your R & D expenditures will result in a technological breakthrough. (When you achieve an R & D breakthrough, you will be given a description of the nature of the breakthrough just below the R & D Index.) This will allow all of your company's models to enjoy an increase in customer preference that will result in an increase in sales. This means that even models that were ranked first in consumer preference before the breakthrough are now preferred even more by consumers. This increase in consumer preference will be known only to you, and you will be notified of it by the increase in your R & D index. The marketing research studies for these four models will still show that they are first, first, second, and second in consumer preference in the four submarkets.

Your decision to spend money on R & D should depend on several factors. Do you have the cash to support R & D expenditures? Are you confident that you already have the models with the greatest customer demand? Are your competitors improving customer demand for their sets by investing in R & D?

Finally, there is no "right" or "wrong" way of handling R & D strategy. Sometimes companies are rewarded by investing in R & D; sometimes they are not. Your company's overall marketing strategy should help you determine whether or not you will invest in R & D.

CHANNEL STRATEGY

A distribution channel for products may be thought of as the series of institutions through which goods or services flow from the point of production to the point of consumption. TVs, for example, are produced by TV manufacturers and then sold to independent retailers (or retail chains) which then sell the sets for ultimate consumption—to the consumer. The "channel" in this case would go from TV manufacturer to retailer to consumer. For any given industry there are many types of channels, that is, many combinations of different institutions. Basically, distribution channel strategy is concerned with the type and number of institutions in the distribution channel and the functions each performs in getting the product to the customers in the target market. The following are examples of some common distribution channels:

Manufacturer	Manufacturer	Manufacturer	Manufacturer
to	to	to	to
Consumer	Retailer	Wholesaler	Agent
	to	to	to
	Consumer	Retailer	Wholesaler
		to	to
		Consumer	Retailer
			to
			Consumer

Companies usually seek the distribution channel that is most efficient—that operates with the lowest costs. Manufacturers may distribute through wholesalers to retailers to consumers. Or they may sell directly to retailers, which, in turn, sell to consumers. Some manufacturers distribute their products directly to consumers via door-to-door salespeople or catalogs. The most efficient channel varies from one industry to another. While there is some variation in the channels used within an industry, over time most firms adopt the most efficient channel structure. Consequently in mature industries almost all of the companies use similar distribution channels.

Once a decision has been made regarding the basic type of channel, another decision must be made regarding the types of channel members a company desires. Suppose a TV manufacturer has decided to distribute to retail dealers, which will then sell the sets to customers. What types of retailers should be selected: department stores, discount stores, variety stores, specialty shops? And will the retailers that are selected agree to carry the manufacturer's sets?

Another decision must be made regarding how many members to have in the distribution channel. Consider an automobile firm. Auto firms must know that they are more likely to sell large numbers of autos in a town if they have a dealer in that town. But in determining the channel strategy for the auto firm the marketing executive must always ask, "Will an additional dealer in Anytown, U.S.A. be profitable?" You must realize that there are costs associated with adding and maintaining dealers in a distribution channel. As a general rule, the more dealers there are, the greater the sales, . . . and the greater the operating expenses.

Of course many other decisions must be made regarding distribution channels. Setting the terms and responsibilities of the channel members and evaluating and controlling their performance are but a few of the dimensions of channel strategy that are beyond the scope of this book.

Channel Strategy in Marketing Simulation

Your company is a manufacturer of television sets. You spend money to identify the types of television sets today's consumers want; you spend money on R & D to develop new features; you spend money to promote your sets; and you may distribute your sets to various types of retail dealers, which will then sell your sets to ultimate consumers. Your distribution channel, then, is from manufacturer to retailer to consumer.

In **Marketing Simulation** your channel decisions will be to determine the types of dealers you want to distribute your models to consumers in your target markets and how many of these channel members you want. There are four different types of dealers through which you may decide to distribute your sets. They are (1) furniture stores, (2) TV specialty stores, (3) discount stores, and (4) department stores. These dealers are distributed fairly equally throughout the United States. Though their sales vary slightly from year to year, recent sales figures for these four types of dealers indicate that their percentages of total industry sales are as follows: furniture stores, 10 percent; TV specialty stores, 40 percent; discount stores, 20 percent; and department stores, 30 percent.

In the first quarter of operation your company will start out with 400 dealers, allocated among the four types according to their past sales percentages. Therefore, your company starts with 40 furniture store dealers, 160 TV specialty store dealers, 80 discount store dealers, and 120 department store dealers. You may reallocate these dealers any way you choose without charge only in your first decision. Thereafter there will be an expense of $500 per dealer moved, and this shift will be entered as a dealer change expense on your income statement. Your present allocation of dealers would be shown on your management decision form as follows:

DEALER ALLOCATION
Furniture Store   40
TV Specialty Store 160
Discount Store   80
Department Store 120

If you desire to keep this allocation of dealers, you must complete your management decision form as shown here each time you make a decision. For example, if you want to keep this allocation for Year 1, Quarter 1, you should enter the same number of dealers shown here. Any deviation from these numbers indicates to the computer that you are changing your dealer allocation. Failure to place any numbers in these spaces indicates to the computer that you do not want any dealers! This, of course, would be disastrous to your sales. You may access DAT to view your dealer allocation per quarter. Select the History command and then select Dealers.

Companies provide services to their dealers and continually expend funds to pay for these services. For example, communications must be established to inform dealers of price changes, warranty service agreements, or other company policies. Also, companies often provide training programs for dealers and their employees in order to develop their sales and service skills. All of these services are required for a healthy and competitive dealer network in the television industry, and you must spend $125 per dealer per quarter to maintain them. This expense will automatically be placed on your income statement under operating expenses and will be calculated by multiplying $125 times the total number of dealers you have in operation during any given quarter. This item will be labeled Dealer Expense. By accessing DAT you will be able to use a template that will enable you quickly to calculate total dealer expenses with a proposed change in your total number and/or dealer allocation. Select Go and at the master menu select Templates, then Dealer Expenses. Complete the template. Remember, if you make an error, restart by selecting Alt-R.

It is important to remember that you may change the number of dealers you have any time you desire. For example, you may want to increase the number of dealers you have in the TV specialty store category. You may simply increase your total number of dealers by adding more dealers in the TV Specialty Stores category on your management decision form. If you wanted to increase your number of TV specialty store dealers by, say, 10 dealers, you would complete your decision form as follows:

DEALER ALLOCATION
Furniture Store   40
TV Specialty Store 170
Discount Store   80
Department Store   120

This entry means that you now have 170 TV specialty store dealers—10 more than your original allocation of 160.

You may also wish to shift dealers from one type to another. For example, if you think your company has too many dealers in the TV specialty store category and you believe you do not have enough dealers in the furniture store category, you may simply reduce the number of dealers in the former and add the same number to the latter. This would not result in an increase or decrease in your dealer total, but it could constitute a shift.

As an example of implementing a dealer shift on your Management Decision Form, assume that you decide to shift 20 dealers from TV specialty stores to furniture stores. You should complete your decision form as follows:

DEALER ALLOCATION
- Furniture Store 60
- TV Specialty Store 150
- Discount Store 80
- Department Store 120

Finally, you may want to simply reduce the number of dealers you have in any category. You may even want to reduce the number of dealers in a particular category to 0. Dealer decreases may be made by simply lowering the number of dealers you have in that category. For example, should you want to decrease your department store dealers by 25 dealers, your entry would be as follows:

DEALER ALLOCATION
- Furniture Store 40
- TV Specialty Store 160
- Discount Store 80
- Department Store 95

You should be aware that, realistically, a company does not increase, shift, or decrease its dealers overnight. For this reason, when you add a dealer it takes one additional period for that dealer to operate as effectively as your established dealers. In the long run, then, your established dealers are your more effective dealers. It will cost you $500 to add, shift, or drop a dealer. These expenses will be shown on your income statement as dealer change expenses. You may make all of these changes—dropping, adding, and shifting dealers—simultaneously. You should keep a record of these changes on your distribution expense planning form.

As mentioned previously, your company and all of your competitors start with the same number of dealers (400) allocated over the four types. This number is arbitrary: there is no minimum or maximum number allowable. Why, then, would you want to change? There are several reasons. First, your competitors may add more dealers and thereby gain a competitive edge over your company. Second, you may find that your competitors shift or decrease their dealers in a certain category and that your company may gain a competitive edge by adding more dealers in that particular category. (You will be able to purchase marketing research studies on the types and numbers of dealers used by your competitors. This is explained in Chapter 4.) There are other reasons that you may want to change your number of dealers. These should become apparent during the course of the simulation as your decision-making skills develop.

PRICING STRATEGY

Setting the price of a product or service is a very important part of a company's marketing strategy. The basic price affects the market segment that will be attracted to the product, the support the product will receive from channel members, what types of channel members will distribute the product, and of course the gross revenue and profits a company will receive from any given product. A firm's pricing strategy should consider (1) the level at which the basic prices will be set, (2) how flexible the prices will be, (3) how the firm will react to competitors' price changes, (4) to whom price discounts will be allowed, and (5) legal aspects of the pricing policy. A more complete discussion of pricing strategy can be found in most marketing textbooks.

Pricing Objectives

As stated earlier, before marketing managers can do a job properly, they need objectives. This is true of your pricing strategy decisions as well. Some common pricing objectives are discussed in the following paragraphs.

Achieve a Target Return on Net Sales or Investment. Many companies attempt to achieve a stated "target" return on their investment (or, sometimes, their net sales), such as "20 percent of investment before taxes." Prices on all products are set in such a way as to achieve the "target" return.

Maintain or Improve Market Share. Market share is a valid marketing objective. (Market share, or your percent of the market, is calculated for you and will be included in your Sales Information Printout.) Many companies use pricing strategy as a tool for achieving market share. One national coffee company drops its prices in markets where new competitive coffee brands are being introduced. The purpose is to discourage brand switching by their loyal customers. This pricing strategy enables the company to maintain its market share even in the face of new competitive entries into the market.

Meet Competition. Many companies base their pricing strategy on what their competitors do. National Steel and Kroger, for example, use a "follow-the-leader" policy in making their pricing decisions. They watch for price changes by other dominant companies in their industry, then adjust their prices to meet the competition.

Pricing Strategies: Discount, Premium, and At the Market

Three example basic strategies in marketing are discount pricing, premium pricing, and pricing at the market. **Discount** pricing refers to a strategy of setting prices as low as possible. This enables the company to sell large quantities, thus "penetrating" a sizable percentage of the market. Discount pricing is generally consistent with the strategy of selling large volumes with low markups. However, it requires a very large volume of sales to break even, and it sometimes leads to deadly price wars.

Premium pricing refers to a strategy of setting prices at fairly high pricing points. At high pricing points only a relatively small percentage of potential customers are likely to purchase the product. Therefore premium pricing is generally consistent with the strategy of selling relatively low volumes but achieving substantial profits through high markups. The disadvantage of a premium policy is that it is very susceptible to competitive pricing strategy—it is easy for competitors to enter the market simply by undercutting the "premium" price. However, the effects of competitive retaliation are minimized if the firm's other marketing variables (product, distribution, and promotion) are attractive to customers.

Pricing at the market is another option. With this strategy, a company tries to price its product at the market average or "standard" price. This is a middle-of-the-road strategy seen in industries in which price leadership prevails or buyers have grown used to a customary price for most brands. It effectively takes price out of the marketing strategy equation.

Your pricing decisions will be difficult. To aid you in making these decisions, a section on profit planning is included in this chapter, and we have provided a break-even analysis routine on your DAT. Study both carefully. Profit planning can be very helpful in determining basic pricing points from which to start when developing your pricing strategy.

Pricing Strategy in Marketing Simulation

The price you set on a particular model is the price at which you will sell that model to your dealers—not consumers. You may assume that the lower your price to your dealers, the lower their retail price to their consumers and the greater the volume of dealer sales. Of course if your dealers sell more units, you will sell more units. In other words, you should not concern yourself with pricing at the retail level. If you price your set to a dealer at $1 below the wholesale price on a competing set, you may assume that your retail price will be $1 lower than your competitors'. Each type of dealer, then, marks up the sets by an identical amount.

Your pricing decisions must be made each quarter for each model on the Management Decision Form. This is explained in Appendix B. Remember, the price you enter on the Management Decision Form is the price at which you will sell to your dealers—it is not a retail price. Again, you are reminded not to let judgments based on real-world TV prices influence your pricing decisions.

The computer program is designed to detect exorbitant prices that could result from either collusion or monopoly. If you have a monopoly—that is, if you are the only firm marketing in a given submarket—extremely high prices will probably force your customers to purchase sets designed for other submarkets.

In setting your prices to your dealers, you should keep in mind that the "cost" per model shown in the model description chart represents only the cost of physically producing the set. This figure does not include administrative overhead, depreciation, dealer expenses, promotional expenses, and so forth, which ultimately should be allocated over each unit produced. Certain expenses, such as administrative overhead, have already been determined and will not change. Others, such as promotion, marketing research expenses, and dealer expenses, are determined each quarter by your decisions. Therefore, it is important to keep these decisions in mind when determining your prices to your dealers. Of course you should include some additional margin in the total cost per unit to allow for profit!

Setting price is a critical decision for any business, for it has direct consequences on profit. Over the years, managers have developed helpful tools to assist them in setting prices. Perhaps the most used tool is Break-Even Analysis, while another one is Profit Planning. Both are described in the following paragraphs.

Break-Even Analysis. When considering what prices to charge, you should make some estimate of how the new prices will affect your demand. Break-even analysis is a useful tool here, for it tells you the amount of unit sales necessary to cover your costs exactly. Any sales level above the break-even point will result in profit, while any sales level below it will yield a net loss.

To perform break-even analysis, you only need to know three things. First, you must determine your fixed costs. These are the costs incurred by your company every quarter independent of your production and sales levels. In **Marketing Simulation**, they are identified as your operating expenses on your income statement. Because you are marketing four different products, you need to decide on how much of the total fixed costs will be allocated to each product. One handy means is to use the percent of total dollar sales accounted for by that product, which is calculated for you and appears as part of your Profit Analysis information (see sample printouts in Appendix D).

The second item necessary to perform break-even analysis is the variable cost per unit. This amount pertains to raw materials, labor, and other costs directly related to the production of a product. These costs were provided earlier in Table 3.2, identified as your Cost of Production for whichever models you choose to sell.

The third factor in the break-even equation is your intended price level. Now we are ready to calculate the break-even point. Here is the formula:

$$\text{Break-Even Sales in Units} = \frac{\text{Allocated Fixed Costs}}{(\text{Selling Price} - \text{Variable Cost/Unit})}$$

Sometimes the difference between the selling price and the variable cost per unit is referred to as the "contribution margin." So break-even sales in units is equal to allocated fixed costs divided by the contribution margin.

How do you use break-even analysis? It's easy. First decide on your marketing strategy and the appropriate mix (promotion, sales force, and so forth) for next period. Estimate your fixed costs based on that strategy. Multiply the fixed costs number by the percent allocation for that product. Next, determine your variable costs per unit for the product.

Finally, make a forecast of what you anticipate that product's sales will be at a given price. Calculate the break-even point, and compare it to the forecast. If the break-even point is smaller than the forecast, you can expect a profit. But if it is larger than the forecast, you are warned that the price will not be profitable. You need to reconsider your price level or use other marketing variables to increase the demand for your product. If you do the latter, don't forget that your fixed costs will be affected, and you will need to cycle back through the steps we just described to obtain a new break-even point. The break-even analysis routine provided on the DAT section of your DSS will permit you to experiment with various prices to see their effects on the level of sales necessary to just cover costs. To access the break-even analysis template in DAT, enter Go and at the master menu enter Breakeven. All calculations are made after you enter the required information.

Profit Planning. Profit planning is necessary to determine the effects of your pricing decisions on profitability. The Profit Planning Form, Form 4 in Appendix C, has been computerized and is available as part of your DAT. (You access this form on DAT by selecting Templates at the master menu. Then select Profit Planning.) You will find this form to be useful in making your pricing decisions. This form may be used to forecast profits for a particular pricing decision. If you forecast correctly, your entries on this form should approximate the entries on your income statement.

To use the Profit Planning Form you must first determine the number of units you expect to sell at the price you plan to charge. Multiplying the forecast sales by the price gives you the sales revenue for each model. The total sales revenue equals gross sales. Next compute the cost of sales. On this form, cost of sales is determined by multiplying the forecast sales by the production cost per unit listed in the model description chart. This production cost does not include any charge for storage or overtime production. If you forecast accurately, these charges will be minimal. However, if you wish to include a provision for these charges, simply increase the production cost per unit by some reasonable amount. The total of production cost equals cost of sales.

Subtracting cost of sales from gross sales results in gross margin. Gross margin represents the amount of revenue available to pay your operating expenses. Operating expenses are easily determined once you've made your other marketing decisions—dealer expenses, R & D, and so forth. Recall that other templates are available on your DAT to aid you in determining the total costs to be incurred in these other expense categories. Also, don't forget, marketing research expense is expensed in the quarter in which you use the information. Therefore this quarter's marketing research expense is the cost of the research you requested last quarter. Model change expense is incurred only if you changed models at the beginning of the year (after the first year of simulation). The cost is $25,000 per quarter per model changed. Administration expenses are $20,000 per quarter, and depreciation expense is $24,000 per quarter. If your Sources and Uses of Funds Form, Form 6, indicates a cash shortage, your interest expense can be determined by multiplying the amount of accounts payable by 0.04.

Subtracting the total of all operating expenses from gross margin yields income before taxes. Taxes are computed using a tax rate of 50 percent and are subtracted from income before taxes to get income after taxes. Income after taxes represents your estimated profits for a given pricing decision. To compute earnings per share, divide income after taxes by 100,000 shares.

The Profit Planning Form can be used in this way to analyze the effect of various combinations of sales forecasts, prices, and expenses on profits. Remember, your profit estimate will be only as accurate as your sales forecast. Therefore it is important that you realistically analyze the effects of your pricing decisions on the expected level of sales.

You will notice that this section is similar to the Understanding Your Income Statement section in Appendix A. Profit planning, however is undertaken *before* you implement your decision for any given quarter. It represents your profit/cost *objectives*. The income statement represents your actual *results* and should be analyzed carefully when you make future profit planning estimates. In fact, it would be useful to compare your actual income statement with a printed copy of your Profit Planning Form. Since the latter represents objectives, you can compare it with your results. This will be a meaningful diagnostic exercise.

Profit Analysis. For each period you will be provided with a profit analysis in the lower section of your Balance Sheet Printout. The purpose of the profit analysis is to analyze the profitability of each TV model marketed. To do this the gross margin per unit is computed by taking the difference between sales revenue for a model and the cost of sales for that model and dividing it by the number of unit sales.

From gross margin per unit we subtract operating expenses per unit. Since most of the operating expenses cannot be directly charged to a particular model (exceptions are promotion expense and model change expense), the expenses must be allocated according to some formula. The basis for allocating operating expenses to a model in **Marketing Simulation** is the fraction of the company's total dollar sales for that model. (This is calculated for you in the Profit Analysis printout.) Therefore the operating expenses per unit are determined by summing promotion + model change expense + (all other operating expenses multiplied by the fraction of total dollar sales) and dividing the sum by unit sales.

The difference between gross margin per unit and operating expenses per unit is profit per unit. This information will be helpful in assessing the profitability of your marketing strategy for each of the models you market.

PROMOTION STRATEGY

Marketing companies must *communicate* with various publics—suppliers, dealers, government, labor, and of course the consumer. **Promotion** is the term used to describe a number of activities designed to communicate informative and persuasive messages. The overall goal of promotional activities is to stimulate demand for the company's product. Promotional activities are undertaken to make the target market more sensitive to the firm's marketing mix and less sensitive to those of competitors.

Promotion mix is the term used to describe a company's unique combination of the elements of promotion—personal selling, advertising, publicity, and sales promotions. Advertising is any paid, nonpersonal presentation of ideas, goods, or services by an identifiable sponsor. Advertising messages are channeled to consumers through various media including TV, radio, magazines, and newspapers. Personal selling is any paid, personal presentation of ideas, goods, or services by an identifiable sponsor. Personal salespersons are used to communicate messages to dealers as well as ultimate consumers. A personal sales message has a major advantage over other forms of promotion in that the salesperson can answer a customer's questions or objections, and determine exactly what an individual customer's needs may be. Therefore, personal sales presentations are very effective for closing sales. However, they are usually more expensive on a per customer basis, than other forms of promotion. The third form of promotion, sales promotion, includes a variety of persuasive techniques such as window streamers, banners, in-store displays, games, samples, premiums or gifts, and so on. The final major form of promotion is publicity. Publicity is communication about a firm, its products, employees, and so forth, that is not paid for in the sense of buying newspaper space or TV time. Rather, the message is communicated in the media because it is newsworthy or is in some other way significant to the community. A firm having 100 percent employee participation in a community's charity drive will probably receive publicity in the form of a newspaper story. A firm that produces an innovative and radically new product may receive publicity in the form of a cover story in a national magazine. Each element of the promotion mix has different advantages and disadvantages. The interested student may want to refer to a marketing or promotion textbook to learn more about the elements of promotion.

A company's promotion strategy may involve large sums of money spent on all forms of promotion. Another company may spend virtually nothing on promotion but may spend heavily on other marketing mix variables. Hershey, the makers of Hershey candy bars, followed this strategy for many years and was very successful even though it did not advertise.

DETERMINING THE PROMOTION BUDGET

As a general rule, the more you spend on promotion, the more you sell. You should be aware, however, that promotion *alone* is not enough to produce a large volume of repeat sales. Customers ultimately must be satisfied with the total marketing mix: the product itself, the price, and the place where the product was purchased.

Economics teaches us that we should spend dollars on promotion until marginal cost equals marginal revenue (MC = MR). However, it is difficult to measure the marginal revenue that results from a promotional expenditure because sales dollars are a function of all four of the marketing mix variables. Marginal analysis does teach us some useful notions, however, concerning optimizing returns from expenditures. For example, we learn from marginal analysis that very small expenditures on promotion (we could apply the same logic to other business expenses) are not likely to have an appreciable effect on increasing sales revenue. Furthermore, at some higher level of expenditure, sales should begin to increase at an increasing rate; and at some still higher level of expenditure, sales revenue will begin to level off. Finally, at some very high level of expenditure, you will be "throwing dollars away" because incremental promotional expenses will not return an equal level of incremental sales revenue. While this theory does not tell you how many dollars to allocate to promotion, distribution, and so forth, it should provide you with the fundamental frame of reference necessary to make near-optimal business decisions.

Marketers commonly use one or a combination of methods to set their promotional budgets. The major methods are summarized in the following paragraphs.

1. *A fixed percentage of sales* or profits is often used to set a promotion budget. A company names a fixed percentage (say, 3 percent) of either sales or profits, and this is used to set the promotional budget. The advantage of this approach is that it is easy to calculate. It has serious disadvantages, however, in that it does not consider the future marketing environment—the budget is set on the basis of past sales or past profits. Also, an increase in promotional expenditures may be required to offset declines in sales or profits. Yet this approach dictates a decrease in promotion expenditures if sales are declining.
2. *The need to meet competition* is often the basis of a promotional budget. Companies strive to spend as much as their competitors or, in some instances, more than their competitors. The fallacy here is that the competition frequently does not know how much should be spent on promotion either. Also, it is often difficult to determine what competitors are spending on promotion. The amount a company claims to spend on promotion often differs greatly from the amount it actually spends.
3. *A task or objective* approach is sometimes used. A company sets itself a task or objective—to increase market share, to enter a new market, or whatever—and then determines how much promotional expenditure is required to meet the objective or perform the task. This approach is much more sound than the two previous approaches. It is more difficult to implement, however, because it does not lend itself to simple and rapid calculations. Determining how much promotional expenditure is required for a given task or objective can be time-consuming and difficult even for an experienced marketer.

There is another promotion concept that you should know. One of the reasons that it is so difficult to measure the effectiveness of promotion is that it has "lagged effects." That is, the purchase of a Zenith TV set today may have been influenced to a large extent by advertisements paid for last year. The effect of a promotional message carries over into the future. A firm that spends $2 million on promotion this year knows that the effects of this spending will be felt for several years.

Promotion Strategy in Marketing Simulation

Companies in the television industry spend large sums of money on almost all of the various forms of promotion. A company may advertise in almost all kinds of media, maintain its own personal sales force, participate in sales promotions, and lease space at national and regional trade shows. In **Marketing Simulation** you will be able to allocate your promotional expenditures to:

Advertising
- TV advertising
- Magazine advertising
- Newspaper advertising

Sales promotions (in-store displays, window signs, banners, and so forth)

Personal selling

You may allocate promotional dollars to any, or all, of these forms of promotion. You will be able to allocate advertising and sales promotion dollars for each model you produce and market. By totaling all these expenditures you will have one promotion expense which will be itemized as "promotion" in the operating expenses portion of your income statement. It is recommended that you first determine how much you want to spend on promotion (set the promotional budget, that is). Then determine how you wish to allocate this budget to the four elements of the promotion mix in **Marketing Simulation** for each TV model you are marketing.

For **personal selling** you will be able to determine the size of your sales force. Each salesperson will call on all types of your dealers and will be knowledgeable about all the models you are producing. You will begin simulation play with 10 salespeople. When you add a salesperson there will be a one-time recruiting and training expense of $5,000. Note that you will be able to enter the total number of salespersons you desire on your Management Decision Form and the total number of salespersons you have will be reported to you on your Sales Information Printout. Furthermore, because it will take one quarter to fully train each salesperson, you will not receive any sales benefits from the new salesperson until the quarter following the quarter in which he or she was hired. You will be able to fire salespersons. There will be a one-time severance fee of $3,000. Finally, you will pay all salespersons a salary of $3,000 per month. All expenses incurred due to hiring, firing, and salaries will be reported to you under the operating expenses section of your income statement as "personal selling" expense. Since you currently have 10 salespersons you have a charge of $90,000 for personal selling on your last quarter's income statement (10 salespersons X $3,000 X 3 months). (See Table 2.1.)

You can assume that you will receive more orders for your TV models the more you spend on promotion. When you promote your TV brand you attract consumers to your dealer outlets, and the more your dealers sell, the more you will sell. Once again, however, you are cautioned that in the area of promotional expenditures there is a point beyond which you are "throwing you money away." The optimum level of your promotional expenditures will depend to a large extent on how much your four competitors are spending. You will be able to purchase marketing research studies on the promotion expenditures of your competition. (These are explained in Chapter 4.)

Business decision makers know that promotional expenditures affect not only present sales but future sales as well. Therefore not only will your present promotional expenditures affect sales but your past promotional expenditures will also carry over to present sales. Realistically, the exact amount of this carry-over effect is never known with certainty. When playing **Marketing Simulation** you will not know exactly what effects your past promotion is having on present sales, but you should be aware that this "lagged" relationship exists in the game as well as in the real world.

You will actually implement your promotion expenditure decision for each TV model by filling in the appropriate spaces on the Management Decision Form. This form is explained fully in Appendix B.

Chapter 4
Marketing Research

The purpose of marketing research is to provide decision makers with information that will enable them to make better decisions. To help you make decisions in **Marketing Simulation** you may wish to purchase certain marketing research studies. These studies are described in the following paragraphs.

Marketing research is purchased in *advance* of making a decision. (What good would the information be to you *after* you have made your decision?) To begin your simulation play you will probably want to buy marketing research studies to aid in making your first set of decisions. The Marketing Research Request Form (see Form 2 in Appendix C) is the first form you will complete and submit to your instructor. When you receive the research information you have requested you will be in a position to make your first decision. (This, of course, assumes that you will want to buy marketing research. You do not have to purchase research, and indeed, much research information that is relevant to your first decision is already available in this book. Do you know what it is?)

After you have received your first research information on your Marketing Research Results Printout and are ready to make your first set of management decisions (for Year 1, Quarter 1), you may also want to turn in another request for marketing research so that when you receive the results of your decisions you will also receive research information to help you make your decisions for Year 1, Quarter 2. You always request marketing research information one quarter in advance.

All marketing research is paid for one quarter *after* it is ordered. In other words, your first task will be to decide what research information you want. However, the research you buy will not be paid for until you make your first management decision. In other words, the marketing research you buy for your Year 1, Quarter 0 will be expensed on your Year 1, Quarter 1 income statement. When you request research at the time you turn in your Year 1, Quarter 1 decisions, these expenses will appear on your Year 1, Quarter 2 income statement, and so on.

As explained in Appendix B, when you select the Marketing Research Request Form from the menu on your DSS Disk, the form will appear on your computer screen. You will be prompted to enter the number that designates the study you wish to buy. When you enter that number you will observe that you will toggle the N in the right column to a Y. The Y means you are buying the study. If you change your mind all you need do is, once again, enter the study number and toggle the Y back to an N. PLEASE NOTE: once you toggle the Y on you will continue buying that study in future quarters unless, as you make your decisions in the subsequent quarter, you toggle the Y back to an N.

QUARTERLY SALES FORECAST

One of your major tasks is to forecast demand and determine the number of units of each model you wish to produce. To help you do this you may want to get some estimate of the number of units that will be sold in the television industry in the coming quarter, by submarket. A marketing research firm will provide you with a quarterly sales forecast that will give you a rough estimate of total industry sales in each submarket for the coming quarter. This forecast will usually be within 5 percent of the true industry's quarterly sales potential. The firm will charge you $20,000 to conduct this study. To buy this forecast you simply toggle on the Y by entering the number of the study. (An N indicates that you do not want the study.) Your information will appear on your Marketing Research Printout in the following form:

```
ESTIMATED SALES FOR YEAR _____      QUARTER _____
    SUBMARKET 1                   5191.
    SUBMARKET 2                   7787.
    SUBMARKET 3                   3894.
    SUBMARKET 4                   15574.
```

The remaining market research information that is available to you is composed of studies of your competition or consumer preference studies of the various TV models.

COMPETITIVE-DEALER STUDIES

You may find that you know almost everything about your competition yet are not making satisfactory profits. If so, you may have overlooked a key source of competitive marketing strategy—the number and types of dealers used by your competition. This may put you at a competitive disadvantage, and therefore you may want to determine just how many and what types of dealers your competitors have. Marketing research can help you answer these questions. If you want to determine the number of dealers your competitors have, you may buy the Number of Dealers by Company study at a cost of $5000. Your information will appear in the following form on your Marketing Research Results Printout:

NUMBER OF DEALERS BY COMPANY

COMPANY	DEALERS
1	400
2	400
3	400
4	400
5	400

Should you want to determine *both* the number *and* the type of dealers, you may buy the Number of Dealers by Channel by Company study at a cost of $20,000. This information would appear on your Marketing Research Results Printout as follows:

NUMBER OF DEALERS BY CHANNEL BY COMPANY

COMPANY	FURNITURE	TV-SP	DISCOUNT	DEPT
1	40	160	80	120
2	40	160	80	120
3	40	160	80	120
4	40	160	80	120
5	40	160	80	120

COMPETITIVE-PROMOTION STUDIES

You will probably learn that promotion is an often-used form of competitive marketing strategy, and you will constantly want to know how much your company should be spending on promotion. Unfortunately, there is no easy answer to this question, but many firms try to find out what their competitors are spending before they decide on their own promotional strategy. The marketing research firm offers you this information in the Promotion Expenditures by Company study at a cost of $5000. This information will appear on your Marketing Research Results Printout as follows:

PROMOTION EXPENDITURES BY COMPANY

COMPANY	EXPENDITURES
1	80000.
2	80000.
3	80000.
4	80000.
5	80000.

In addition, you may need to know how much is being spent on promotion in each of the four submarkets. You may buy this information by placing a Y in the appropriate space for the Promotion Expenditures by Submarket by Company study on the Marketing Research Request Form. (If you do not want this study place an N in the space.) The cost of this study is $20,000, and the information will appear on your Marketing Research Results Printout as follows:

PROMOTION EXPENDITURES BY SUBMARKET BY COMPANY

COMPANY	SUB-MARKET 1	SUB-MARKET 2	SUB-MARKET 3	SUB-MARKET 4
1	20000.	20000.	20000.	20000.
2	20000.	20000.	20000.	20000.
3	20000.	20000.	20000.	20000.
4	20000.	20000.	20000.	20000.
5	20000.	20000.	20000.	20000.

Finally, you may desire to know not only how much your competitors are promoting in each submarket but how they are allocating their promotion to the various elements of the promotional mix. You may purchase this Current Promotion Expenditures by Submarket by Medium by Company study on the Marketing Research Request Form. The cost of this study is $25,000, and the information will appear on your Marketing Research Results Printout as follows:

PROMOTION EXPENDITURES BY SUBMARKET BY MEDIUM BY COMPANY

TV ADVERTISING

COMPANY	SUB-MARKET 1	SUB-MARKET 2	SUB-MARKET 3	SUB-MARKET 4
1	5000.	5000.	5000.	5000.
2	5000.	5000.	5000.	5000.
3	5000.	5000.	5000.	5000.
4	5000.	5000.	5000.	5000.
5	5000.	5000.	5000.	5000.

... and so on for each medium.

STUDY OF COMPETITORS' SALES FORCE SIZE

You may purchase a study that gives you the number of salespersons active in each company during the quarter the information is requested. The cost of this study is $15,000.

STUDIES OF COMPETITORS' R & D

As discussed previously, expenditures for R & D may be a viable means of increasing customer preference for a company's television sets. You may find that you are having difficulty competing adequately with one or more of your four competitors and your analysis of their models, promotional expenditures, prices, and number and types of dealers may show that all are fairly similar to those of your company. The competitor's advantage, therefore, may be attributed to the technological breakthroughs that it has achieved by spending funds on R & D. To help you determine the amount your competitor is spending on R & D, you may purchase the Cumulative Research and Development Expenditures by Company study from the marketing research firm. This study is available to you at a cost of $5000.

The information that you may obtain from this study will appear on your Marketing Research Results Printout as follows:

CUMULATIVE RESEARCH AND DEVELOPMENT
EXPENDITURES BY COMPANY

COMPANY	EXPENDITURES
1	0
2	0
3	0
4	0
5	0

CONSUMER PREFERENCE STUDIES

You must immediately make a decision regarding which four TV models you will produce. But which models are the best? One way of answering this question is to examine the Model Description Chart (Table 3.2). You may examine the features, cost, submarket, and so forth for each model and *subjectively* determine the "best" four models. ("Best" in this case means those with the greatest consumer appeal or preference.)

If you do not want to make a strictly subjective decision, you may buy consumer preference studies from the marketing research firm. These studies are conducted by surveying a randomly selected sample of consumers. The consumers are shown pictures of the various models and given a brief description of the product features. Two models are tested at a time and the consumer is asked, "Which of the two models do you prefer?" You may buy the results of these studies for all models in a submarket. The cost for *each* submarket study is $30,000.

To better understand these preference studies consider the following example. Suppose that you want to know the consumer preferences for the models in submarket 1. The Model Description Chart provides some information about each of the four models (A, B, C, and D). You do not know, however, how the "consumers" in **Marketing Simulation** prefer the various models. Therefore, you may want to buy this study if you want to market a model or models in submarket 1. If you purchase this preference study, your information will appear on your Marketing Research Results Printout in the following form:

PRODUCT PREFERENCE RATING FOR SUBMARKET 1

55% PREFERRED PRODUCT A TO PRODUCT B
39% PREFERRED PRODUCT A TO PRODUCT C
44% PREFERRED PRODUCT A TO PRODUCT D
44% PREFERRED PRODUCT B TO PRODUCT A
34% PREFERRED PRODUCT B TO PRODUCT C
39% PREFERRED PRODUCT B TO PRODUCT D
60% PREFERRED PRODUCT C TO PRODUCT A
65% PREFERRED PRODUCT C TO PRODUCT B
55% PREFERRED PRODUCT C TO PRODUCT D
55% PREFERRED PRODUCT D TO PRODUCT A
60% PREFERRED PRODUCT D TO PRODUCT B
44% PREFERRED PRODUCT D TO PRODUCT C

    This example shows the type of printout you would receive if you requested a consumer preference study for submarket 1. The cost of this study would be $30,000. This amount would be itemized under marketing research expense on the next income statement you receive after purchasing this research information.

    Be cautioned that you want to market the model in a submarket with the greatest amount of consumer preference. If, by interpreting the results of a consumer preference study, you determine for instance, model C is the most preferred model, you should market model C. Do not be concerned that other firms may also market model C. If you market any other model, your model will have less consumer preference. In order to achieve the same level of sales, you will have to have a lower price, more promotion, more distribution, and so forth.

Chapter 5
Evaluating Your Performance

The function of management is to create an environment in which individuals may work together effectively and efficiently. By "creating an environment" we mean that managers are responsible for taking the assets of the firm and organizing them in such a way that the goals of the organization are effectively and efficiently achieved. The manager of a manufacturing plant, for example, creates the proper environment to achieve production goals by organizing the assets—personnel, machinery, raw materials, and so forth—in a certain fashion. To create and maintain this environment, management must plan what assets are needed and what production objectives must be achieved. Management must also organize the assets so that the right workers are doing the right tasks and so that these workers have the proper tools and supplies. Management also motivates and leads the workers so that they have incentives to work properly. Finally, management must devise a control system that allows for corrective action to be taken in case actual production is less than the planned production objective. So we see that management has several functions—planning, organizing, leading, and controlling. Managers undertake each of these functions in managing an organization. These functions are equally applicable to a manufacturing and marketing firm such as yours. However, while management does undertake several functions, the essential task of management is to create an environment in which individuals may work together effectively and efficiently.

As the marketing management of your television firm you are allowed to "create an environment" by the marketing management decisions you make. You determine what quantities and types of TV sets your firm will produce, the prices of these sets, the dealer network you will use to distribute your sets, the types and levels of promotion, and so forth. You have assets—existing and potential dealers, funds for promotion, an R & D department, production workers, machinery and equipment, and so forth. Your marketing management decisions will result in a unique arrangement of these assets: you have created a certain environment for your firm.

Once you have made your decisions you will want to know whether or not the "environment" you have created will be both effective and efficient. In other words, you are now ready to evaluate your performance as a manager. In order to do this, we must clearly understand the concepts upon which management is evaluated-effectiveness and efficiency.

By "effective" we mean that management meets some stated standard of performance, or a stated objective. Hence, the standard of effectiveness is determined by management as it determines the organization's objectives. If the firm achieves the objective, then management has been effective, by definition. If the firm's performance is below stated objectives, then management has not been effective. If you set a net profit objective of $200,000, for example, and you actually earn a net profit of $205,000, then you have been effective because you achieved your stated goal.

MEASURES OF EFFECTIVENESS

Companies typically select a number of objectives to measure the effectiveness of their management's performance. Common objectives are sales volume, market share, profits before taxes, and net profits. Of course companies may set these objectives for the entire company and/or for different market segments, products, and so on.

Measures of Effectiveness in Marketing Simulation

In **Marketing Simulation** you have an Objectives and Planning Form, Form 1, on which to record your stated objectives. It is recommended that you set specific objectives for each quarter of simulation for at least sales volume, market share, and net profits. You should also consider setting objectives for your expenses as well. Further, since you are likely to be evaluated in terms of your cumulative profit standing within your industry, industry standing in terms of profits may also be a useful goal for you to consider.

To help you evaluate the effectiveness of your performance as well as maintain accurate records, you should consider using a graph similar to that shown in Figure 5.1, Example of Stated Versus Actual Net Profits for Year 1. Of course this example is for the net profit objective but you may want to develop such charts for each of your stated objectives. Many of your actual results will be automatically graphed on your DAT. You will find a review of these graphs, in light of your objectives, will be insightful.

One final note regarding measures of effectiveness should be stated. Any firm's management may be effective if it consistently states low objectives that are easily attained. You should not set your objectives so that they may easily be achieved because, as you will see in the next section, you may be very effective but also very inefficient. Managers must be both effective and efficient. On the other hand, set reasonable objectives that are possible to achieve. The longer you play **Marketing Simulation** the more adept you will become at setting sound, reasonable objectives.

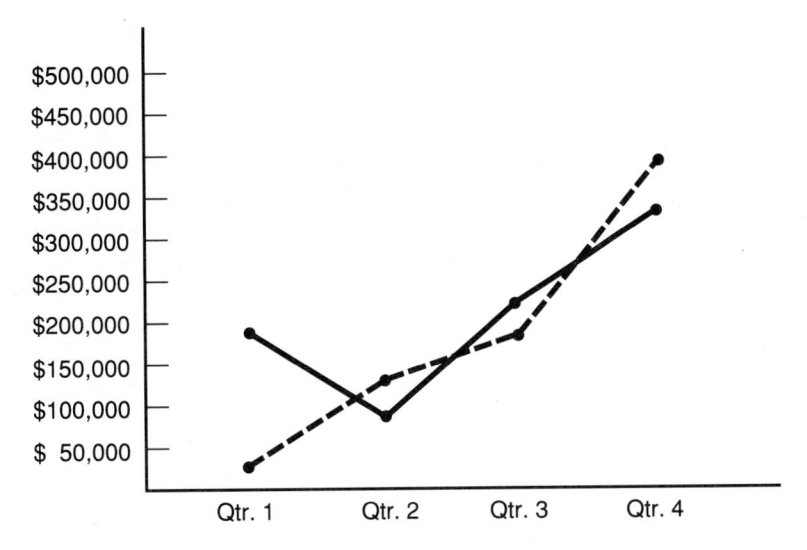

Stated Net Profits = Solid Line: Actual Net Profit = Dashed Line

FIGURE. 5.1
EXAMPLE OF STATED VERSUS ACTUAL NET PROFITS FOR YEAR 1

MEASURES OF EFFICIENCY

Measures of efficiency are also very important in evaluating management's performance. Efficiency is quite different from effectiveness in that efficiency measures a firm's output (i.e., net profits) relative to the inputs (i.e., assets) that were used to generate the output. If, for example, two firms state their net profit objective to be $100,000 for a given quarter and each firm earns in excess of $100,000 during that quarter, then each firm has been effective, by definition. However, what if one firm's management has assets (plant, equipment, machinery, inventory, and so forth) totalling $10 million while the other has assets of only $1 million. The management of the firm with only $1 million in assets has been many times more efficient than the other firm's management. Why? Because they earned the same net income (output) with ten times less assets (inputs). In this example, stockholders may be reasonably pleased with the management of the $1 million firm while the stockholders of the $10 million firm would probably want to fire the management of their firm immediately. Consequently, it is not adequate to assess a management's performance in terms of effectiveness alone. We must assess management's efficiency.

A convenient method of measuring efficiency, which is comparing output relative to input, is ratio analysis. Financial ratio analysis, the application of ratio analysis to financial data, allows us to compare a number of areas of performance simply by dividing output by input. The resulting ratio, or index, generates a measure of efficiency and allows for a better understanding of the performance of the firm. The most commonly used ratio is known as ROI (return on investment). It is calculated by dividing net profits (output) by total assets (input) and the resulting percentage tells the analyst how efficiently the firm is using its assets. Furthermore, it may tell the investors in the firm whether or not they should continue to remain in that particular type of business.

There are two major ways to use ratio analysis. First, you may compare a present ratio with past and expected future ratios for the same company. When financial ratios are compared over several time periods, the analyst can study changes and trends which provide an understanding of a company's performance over time. A second method of using ratio analysis involves comparing the ratios of one firm with those of similar firms or with industry averages at the same point in time. A firm may then determine its performance relative to other similar firms in the same industry. Comparisons of one firm's ratios with those of other firms within the same industry will provide a good yardstick upon which to evaluate a firm's efficiency.

Measures of Efficiency in Marketing Simulation

A large number of financial ratios may be computed for any given company. However, the ratios needed to assess the performance of a company are really relatively few in number. In **Marketing Simulation** you will be able to assess your efficiency with the following ratios: Profit to Sales Ratio, Sales to Asset Turnover, Return on Assets, and Return on Net Worth. (Of course, earnings per share, which has already been discussed, is also a ratio.) Each of these ratios will be calculated for you in the Ratio Analysis section of your printout, which may be found directly below your Income Statement. The Ratio Analysis section will not only give you your firm's own ratios, it will also give you an industry average for each ratio. The following section explains the ratios that will be available to you in **Marketing Simulation**. You will be able to view graphs of your ratios over time by accessing your DAT. Select the History option on the master menu. Start the program and then select Performance. A menu will then appear, giving you a choice of several ratios to review.

Profit to Sales Ratio. The profit to sales ratio is calculated by dividing net profits (Income After Taxes) by sales (Gross Sales):

$$\text{Profit to Sales Ratio} = \frac{\text{Income After Taxes}}{\text{Gross Sales}}$$

The resulting percentage tells you how many dollars and cents of net profit you are earning on each dollar of sales. Therefore, it is a measure of how efficient you are in terms of profitability in relation to sales. A low percentage, for example, may indicate that you are generating a high sales volume by spending large sums on marketing expenses (promotion, distribution, and so forth). Hence, because your expenses are so high your profits per dollar of sales will be low.

Sales to Asset Turnover. Sales to asset turnover is calculated by dividing sales (Gross Sales) by total assets:

$$\text{Sales to Asset Turnover} = \frac{\text{Gross Sales}}{\text{Total Assets}}$$

The resulting percentage tells you how many dollars and cents of sales you generated for each dollar of assets you manage.

Therefore, this ratio tells us the relative efficiency with which the firm utilizes its assets to generate sales. Of course, in **Marketing Simulation**, a large component of your assets is represented by plant and equipment over which you have no control. (You do, however, control inventory and cash). Nevertheless, this ratio is included to help you learn various ratios and how they may be used to evaluate your efficiency.

Return on Investment. Return on investment, also commonly referred to as ROI, is generally regarded as the single most important yardstick by which to measure a firm's performance. It is, unfortunately, widely misunderstood. The purpose of ROI is to provide a measure of the dollars and cents earned per dollar invested and is calculated by dividing net profits (Income After Taxes) by investment. The source of most of the confusion in understanding ROI is in determining how to calculate investment. However, we may easily calculate investment if we know who we are calculating ROI for—the firm's management or the firm's owners (investors).

If we are determining ROI for a firm's management, we are essentially asking, "What amount of dollars and cents did these managers earn for each dollar of assets they managed?" Which assets then, do managers manage? All of them—total assets! Therefore, to evaluate ROI in terms of management's efficiency we calculate a ratio called return on assets (ROA) by dividing net profits (Income After Taxes) by total assets (Total Assets):

$$\text{Return on Assets} = \frac{\text{Net Profits}}{\text{Total Assets}}$$

Second, if we are determining ROI for the owners/investors of a firm we are essentially asking, "What amount of dollars and cents did the owners earn for each dollar they invested in the business?" Now, what represents the dollars that owners have invested in a business? Net Worth! Therefore, to evaluate in terms of the owners' efficiency we calculate a ratio known as return on net worth (RONW) by dividing net profits (Income After Taxes) by net worth (Capital Stock plus Retained Earnings)

$$\text{Return on Net Worth} = \frac{\text{Net Profits}}{\text{Capital Stock} + \text{Retained Earnings}}$$

Certainly there are many other factors of ratio analysis that may be considered but they are beyond the scope of this book. The essential point you should understand is that management should be evaluated in terms of both effectiveness and efficiency. You now have the basic tools necessary to evaluate your performance as a manager in **Marketing Simulation**.

THE DECISION ANALYSIS TOOLS

As you compete in **Marketing Simulation**, you will receive numerous income statements, balance sheets, sales analyses, and marketing research reports. Also, you will find it advantageous to perform break-even analyses, estimate cash flow, and compute expected profit for coming quarters. You, just as managers in the real world, will soon find it a formidable task to manage all of this information.

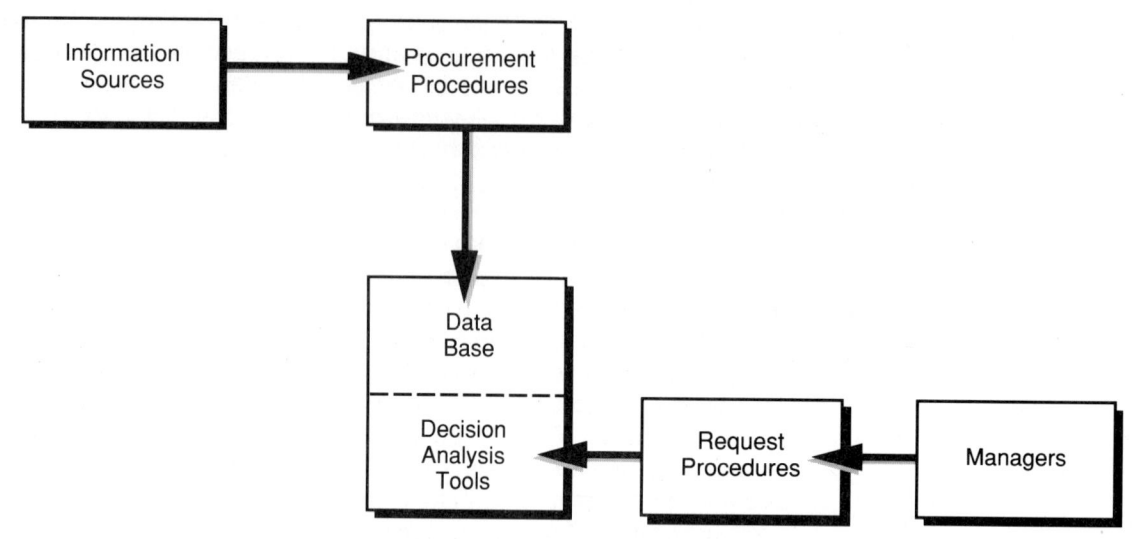

FIGURE 5.2
DIAGRAM OF A MARKETING INFORMATION SYSTEM

Think of information as a source of competitive advantage. If you perceive something in the marketplace and your competition does not, it is possible to use that knowledge to your advantage. For example, if you notice that the market is growing rapidly, and your competitors do not, they will incur overtime charges due to low scheduled production but you will not. If you happen to sell the same amount as your competitor at the same price, you will be more profitable because your costs will be lower.

Many companies recognize the fact that marketplace information has great potential value, and they have invested millions of dollars in the design and operation of systems to provide relevant information to managers when they need it. This is the realm of Marketing Information Systems (MIS). A simple MIS is diagrammed in Figure 5.2.

An MIS is an ongoing system that continually draws in market information, stores it, manipulates it, and presents it to managers in meaningful form upon request. In **Marketing Simulation**, the key information sources provided to all competitors as normal output include income statement figures (sales, costs, profit), inventory status (production, sales, inventory on hand), the financial ratios and measures of effectiveness just described, and sales analyses for each submarket.

We have created an MIS for you, and it is contained on the Student DSS Disk that accompanies your **Marketing Simulation** manual. As you play successive quarters of **Marketing Simulation**, the data base will grow in size, and you may request to look at your past decisions, performance, and comparisons to competitors. This is a valuable resource, and you should strive to familiarize yourself with its various aspects. Remember, the knowledge you glean from this data base could very well be the key to your success in this simulation game.

As we explain in Chapter 1, your DSS consists of two parts, the Decision Input System (DIS) and Decision Analysis Tools (DAT). DIS allows you to enter your decisions directly on your computer screen and view (a hard copy print option is also available) the results of these decisions after the instructor has completed processing.

The DAT are of two types: (1) graphs and (2) analysis forms. For the most part, graphs trace your company over past periods. These may seem simple, but once you find your MIS has sufficient historical data, graphs often crystallize patterns, trends, or relationships that are useful in planning future decisions. Your set of Decision Analysis Tools also contains routines to do repetitive computations for analyses you should perform each period in planning your decisions. These include Break Even Analysis, Profit Planning Form, Sources and Uses of Cash Form, Sales Forecasting and Distribution Expenses Form, all of which we described earlier. Again, real-world managers would have computerized routines such as these as a support system for their repetitive decisions.

The DAT provided with **Marketing Simulation** is a network of templates which are designed for the Lotus 1–2–3 spreadsheet programs. Other Lotus-compatible spreadsheets may work as well. *Everything on your DAT is completely menu-driven;* that is, the programming is done, and all you need to do is respond to the prompts at the top of the computer monitor screen. There are prompts asking you whether or not you want to print out the analyses or save graph files for later printing by Lotus PrintGraph. In other words, you do not need to be proficient in the use of Lotus 1–2–3; all you need to know is how to start up the program.

What is in your DAT? There are several parts to it:

1. Historical Information
2. Competitive Analysis
3. Inventory Analysis
4. Breakeven Analysis
5. Sources and Uses of Cash Form
6. Forecasting
7. Profit Planning Form, and
8. Distribution Expenses Form

Each is described briefly in the following. (The purposes and specifics of most of these forms were described earlier in Chapter 3.)

Historical Information. This part of your DAT allows you to review all of your decisions and their outcomes, across past quarters of simulation play. The menus will guide you if your want to look at various decisions, results such as sales and profit, or financial performance ratios. This routine is the essence of your data base, and by inspecting its many graphs you will be able to visualize the patterns, trends, and relationships we alluded to earlier.

Competitive Analysis. Another part of your DAT compares all competitors on various performance measures such as market share, prices, and units sold by type of dealer. This routine will assist you in identifying the strategies (and their results) of specific competitors.

Inventory Analysis. The DAT also has a routine that will allow you to review your scheduled production, unit sales, and ending inventory quarter by quarter. By inspecting these graphs, you may be able to see opportunities to improve your production scheduling, inventory planning, or sales forecasts.

Break-Even Analysis. A standard method of assessing pricing decisions is through break-even analysis, and we described this technique for you in Chapter 3. What we did not describe is "sensitivity analysis." Sometimes you arrive at a tentative price range to charge, but the exact price is not decided. The DAT has a routine for computing break-even levels of sales at alternative prices. When you provide a "target price," this routine will automatically show you break-even sales in units and dollars of revenue for that price, a 10 percent higher price, and a 10 percent lower price. This information will show you how sensitive the break-even point is to price differences.

Sources and Uses of Cash Form. Businesses are constantly concerned about cash flow, and this form will enable you to determine where your cash is being spent and how much is available in the coming period. We described the cash flow problem in Chapter 3, and this routine does the calculations necessary to estimate cash long- or shortfalls. You will find this routine under the Templates option on the master menu.

Forecasting Routines. As was also described in Chapter 3, your DAT gives you some options regarding forecasting individual model sales for the coming quarter. Based on the past three quarters of sales, you may opt for: (1) an average percent sales change forecast, (2) an exponential smoothing forecast weighting the last quarter at 50 percent and the previous two quarters at 25 percent, or (3) an exponential smoothing forecast with 75 percent and 25 percent weights for last quarter and the previous two quarters, respectively.

Profit Planning Form. As part of your planning, you will want to set a profitability objective. By using this form, you can estimate the total profit anticipated by your prices, sales forecasts, and expected costs. We described the general idea of profit planning in Chapter 3. Here is where your sales forecasts, intended price levels, and cost estimates are combined to determine what will happen to the bottom line—profit. The Profit Planning Form is a vital decision-making tool, for it guides your thinking to its most critical impact point on your company. You will find this routine under the Templates option on the master menu.

Distribution Expenses Form. This form helps you to keep track of your expenses associated with making changes in the number of different types of dealers selling your television models. It shows how these decisions will impact on your Dealer Change and Dealer expenses on your income statement. You will also find this routine under the Templates option on the master menu.

How to Operate Your DAT

Be certain you read carefully all the instructions under the menu items Explain DAT, Overview, Warnings, and Restarting, which appear on the first DAT screen. Read this information before accessing the Go to the master menu option.

As we described in Chapter 1, the second line from the top of your screen is Lotus 1-2-3's Command Line. The third line often contains descriptions of the various commands. All you need to do is to move the cursor over each command on the Command Line, and read the description below. Once you have made a menu selection by pressing Enter, you will automatically be presented with another menu. All routines have options in their menus to go back to earlier menus or to call the Master Menu.

Some forms (Profit Planning, Breakeven, and Uses and Sources of Cash) require you to input values. For these, you will be given a prompt on the Command Line. Simply enter the value and press the Return key. Another prompt will appear to move you through the form, or, if the form is filled, to show you the results. You will always have the option to do the form over if you wish to experiment with different values for any of the input factors.

Your Practice Data Set

The value of much of your DAT is greatest when the data base is rich with information. Just think of an MIS for a company that has several years of experience in its data base. There is a wealth of data to inspect for strategic insights. However, in the first few quarters of play, your data base will have very little historical information. It is as though this company suddenly found itself beset with entirely new competitors and a new economic environment. Past experience becomes irrelevant.

Because of the unique start-up conditions of **Marketing Simulation**, your company does not have any relevant history. So we have provided a Practice Data Set on the Student DSS Disk that accompanies your manual. We have provided you with two years (eight quarters) of information for a fictitious firm, X-1. You should inspect it and use it to become familiar with the DAT. The X-1 Practice Data Set will be automatically read into your DAT whenever you load your DAT *before* you begin playing **Marketing Simulation**. After you begin play, the Practice Data Set will be erased and replaced by the new data on the team disk you submit to your instructor for each period of play. It will be automatically updated with each quarter's information as you play. As you move deeper into game play, and the DAT data base grows, you will find the various routines more and more informative. Again, you should strive to convert this information into competitive advantage.

How to Share the Current Data Base with Other Team Members

As we noted earlier, one Student DSS Disk per team is to be submitted to the Instructor with each period of play. That disk will be returned to your team with updated and current financial forms, marketing research information, and revised data base. All team members should have benefit of the new information, so you should copy it onto their disks. You can do this by following these steps:

For a computer with one floppy drive and a hard disk drive:

1. Put your computer in DOS mode.
2. Type DISKCOPY A: B: and press <Enter>.
3. Put the Team DSS Disk in Drive A as the Source disk and press <enter>.
4. Insert the team member's disk in the drive when prompted by the computer. (It will be referred to as the Target disk.)
5. Follow the prompts.
6. Once the copying is complete, do the same with all other team members' disks. Make certain you label each disk properly with the proper industry and company designation and current year and quarter.

For a computer with two floppy drives:

1. Put your computer in DOS mode.
2. Type DISKCOPY A: B: and press <Enter>.
3. Place the Team DSS Disk in the A: drive as the Source disk.
4. Place the team member's disk in the B: drive as the Target disk.
5. Once the copying is complete, do the same with the other team member's disks.

Now all team members have an updated, current data set, and they can use the updated information on their own Student DSS disks at their convenience. This will allow everyone on the team to analyze this data with their DATs so that they will be able to make more informed decisions in **Marketing Simulation**. Also, in the unlikely event that your Team DSS disk is damaged, you will have duplicates available.

Appendix A
Understanding Your Income Statement and Sources and Uses of Funds Form

THE INCOME STATEMENT

Your instructor will provide you with an income statement for your company every time you make a decision. The disk you select as your Team DSS disk will be returned to you and you will be able to print out your reports, or view them on your computer screen, by selecting the Print Company Reports menu item. The income statement is the best tool for evaluating your decision in terms of profits and costs on a quarterly basis. Your most recent income statement may be found in Table 2.1. In addition, a sample income statement printout is provided in Appendix D as well as on your Student DSS disk (see Print Company Reports). These examples are to help you become familiar with the actual form of this important document.

The income statement is a valuable source of information. Not only does it report the soundness of your past marketing management decisions, it can also help you make strategy decisions for the future. You should review your income statement to analyze certain basic factors. If your performance is poor, for example, you may find that your sales were adequate but your costs were excessive. On the other hand, your costs may be very much in line with acceptable levels, but your sales revenue may not be adequate. The income statement also provides you with information that can help you determine which of your costs, if any, are excessive. Are your storage or overtime costs excessive? Are any of your expense items, such as promotion, dealer expense, or dealer change expense, excessive? Your answers to these and other basic questions should help you determine your strategy. You should turn back to the Objectives section (Chapter 1) to review how your profit and cost objectives are interrelated. The following paragraphs explain how the entries on your

74 Marketing Simulation

income statement are determined. You should go over these explanations carefully and examine the income statement in Appendix D to ensure that you understand the relationships among the various entries on this document.

Sales

Your total sales revenue—Sales—will be the first entry on your income statement. Sales revenue is calculated by multiplying the number of units of a given TV model actually sold during the quarter by your selling price for that model. The Sales will be listed on your income statement for each of your four models. These sales figures will be totaled, yielding your gross sales. Also, since at the end of each year your unsold sets are sold to the industrial market, there will be an entry labeled Industrial Sales during the fourth quarter of each year. This will appear on your Sales Information Printout for the fourth quarter. The dollar value of industrial sales is calculated by multiplying each unit sold by 90 percent of its production cost. Note that since all sets are sold during the fourth quarter, no storage charges will be incurred during the last quarter of each year.

Cost of Sales

The second section of your income statement is designed to help you determine the cost of sales, sometimes called the cost of goods sold. Begin by examining the beginning inventory, which represents the value of the sets that are on hand because they were not sold in the previous quarter. Beginning inventory is determined by the amount shown in ending inventory of the previous quarter's income statement. Remember that all entries on your income statement are in dollar amounts. To determine the number of *units* in inventory, examine the inventory analysis section of the Balance Sheet Printout in Appendix D.

Current production is the second entry under costs of sales. Current production is determined by multiplying the model production cost shown in the Model Description Chart (Table 3.2) by the number of units of each model produced. Remember that you have a minimum production requirement of 2000 units per quarter. This may be allocated among the models any way you like, but the *total* production for all models must be at least 2000 units. If your production request is below the minimum, you will automatically produce an additional number of sets so that you produce a total of 2000 units. The additional units will be produced in proportion to the production allocation for the four models in the previous quarter.

The next item entered under cost of sales is overtime production. You will experience these overtime charges when your sales of any of your four models amount to more than the number of models you currently produce plus the number of models you had in beginning inventory. This simply means that you underestimated the demand for your television sets and that you sold more units than the number you had available for sale. Since your union contract allows you to produce in an overtime situation, you will never have stockouts. However, the overtime charges will result in an additional charge equal to 10 percent of the production cost of each set produced in overtime production. This amount will be entered on your income statement as overtime production and may be determined by multiplying 110 percent by the production cost, shown in the Model Description Chart, of the model produced in overtime.

Should the sales of your sets amount to less than the number of sets you have in current production and the number you had in beginning inventory, you will have sets left over and must store them at a cost of 5 percent of their cost of production. This total charge will be entered on your income statement as storage charge.

The next entry on your income statement will be labeled Available for Sale. This amount is determined by summing the dollar values of beginning inventory, the dollar value of the sets in current production, charges for overtime production (if any), and storage charges (if any). It is important to remember that this entry reflects the dollar value of the sets you have available for sale. It does not tell you how many *units* you have available for sale. If you are not sure how to calculate the number of units you have in inventory, you should reread the Inventory Planning section in Chapter 3.

The next item on your income statement is labeled Ending Inventory. Ending inventory represents the production costs of the television model multiplied by the number of sets that are not sold during the current quarter. The dollar amount represented by ending inventory should be subtracted from the dollar amount available for sale. The difference is the next entry on the income statement, namely, Cost of Sales. Cost of sales represents the production costs, including any overtime or storage charges, of the sets that were actually sold during the quarter. The cost of sales is subtracted from gross sales, and the difference is recorded on your printout as gross margin.

Operating Expenses

All other operating expenses are then subtracted from your gross margin. Certain operating expenses are predetermined and thus are fixed expenses. They are administration ($20,000) and depreciation ($24,000). Other expenses include promotion expense, which you determine each quarter; dealer expense, which is equal to $125 times the number of dealers in your distribution network; dealer change expense, which is equal to $500 times the number of dealers you have added, deleted, or shifted; personal selling expense which includes monthly salaries at $3,000 per salesperson plus $5,000 per salesperson you add to cover recruiting, selection, and training and every time you fire a salesperson you will be charged an additional $3,000 to cover severance expenses; marketing research, which is the cost of any research studies that you purchased in the *previous* quarter; research and development, which is the amount you may have invested in R & D in the present quarter; model change expense, which is a $100,000 expense amortized at $25,000 per quarter and is incurred only if you change one of your TV models *after* you have made your decision for Year 1, Quarter 1; and interest charge, which is equal to 4 percent quarterly (16 percent annually) on any loans made to the company. The amount of those loans will be shown in the accounts payable entry on the balance sheet. (The loans are automatically made in amounts that prevent a company from having a negative cash balance.) Operating expenses are summed and subtracted from the gross margin. The difference is recorded as income before taxes.

Income and Taxes

Income taxes are calculated on your income statement as 50 percent of your income before taxes. However, if your company sustained a loss in a previous period, the amount of the loss is subtracted from income before taxes before the present quarter's tax liabilities are computed. For example, assume that you lost $10,000 last quarter and made income before taxes of $50,000 in the present quarter. Your income taxes would be $20,000. This figure is calculated by subtracting former losses from present income before taxes ($50,000 − $10,000 = $40,000) and multiplying this by 50 percent (0.50 X $40,000 = $20,000).

Tax credits from losses also carry over into future periods if they are not needed in the present period. If you incur a $10,000 loss in one quarter and make a profit of only $5,000 in the following quarter, you have a $5,000 tax credit (to be deducted from the next quarter's income before taxes) that will be carried over to the next quarter of operation.

After income taxes have been calculated, they are subtracted from income before taxes. The difference is income after taxes. Finally, income after taxes is divided by the 100,000 shares of outstanding common stock to yield earnings per share.

THE SOURCES AND USES OF FUNDS FORM

In this section we explain cash flow. You should know where your cash comes from and how you spend it—hence, the name *sources* and *uses* of funds. You are provided with a Sources and Uses of Funds Form, Form 6 in Appendix C, to help you calculate your cash for each quarter. This is computerized for you as a part of your DAT. You may access this computerized form, called Cash Flow, by selecting the Templates option on the master menu. You will be able to enter the values of a proposed decision and the DAT will calculate whether or not you will need cash for the upcoming quarter.

At the beginning of play you have cash on hand in the amount of $438,900. (See the balance sheet in Table 2.2.) The other source of cash is the revenue generated by sales in the current period. As you sell to your dealers you immediately receive cash payments. Therefore your sources of cash are the cash balance on your balance sheet and the gross sales on your income statement. Of course when you are planning for cash flow, you will not yet have gross sales recorded on your income statement. When you are attempting to predict your cash flow for a given proposed decision, you must forecast gross sales.

The uses of cash are (1) current production, including any overtime or storage costs; (2) promotion expense; (3) dealer and dealer change expense; (4) personal selling expenses; (5) marketing research expenditures; (6) research and development expenditures; (7) model change expense; (8) administrative expenses; (9) interest charge; and (10) income taxes.

You determine the amount of cash on hand by subtracting *uses* of funds from *sources* of funds. Should your uses exceed your sources, you have a "cash flow problem"—you need cash! You automatically borrow, in this case, from a bank that charges you 16 percent interest—4 percent per quarter. The amount of this loan will be added to your accounts payable account on your balance sheet, and the interest charge will begin one quarter after the loan is made and will be itemized on your income statement under operating expenses.

If your sources of funds exceed your uses of funds, this cash will be used to (1) reduce your accounts payable account and/or (2) increase your cash account.

You may find that you made a positive net income in a given quarter yet had to borrow money. Usually this situation means that you overproduced, leaving your cash tied up in inventory. Get familiar with the Cash Flow Form on your DAT by accessing the Templates menu option. You will find that this template will make your calculations much simpler.

Appendix B
Completing Your Decision Forms

As a matter of mechanics, it is important that you understand how to implement your marketing strategy decision in **Marketing Simulation**. You have been referring to two forms—the Management Decision Form, Form 3, and the Marketing Research Request Form, Form 2—while reading this book. The following paragraphs provide the additional information you need to use these forms properly. You are provided with blank copies of these forms in Appendix C. Your instructor will give you a choice of either making your decisions on these forms and submitting the forms to her or him, or your instructor may allow you to make you decisions directly on your Student DSS Disk. You would then give one disk, designated the Team DSS, disk in to the instructor for processing. Be sure to copy your Team DSS Disk onto a backup disk each time you make decisions.

THE MARKETING RESEARCH REQUEST FORM

Since the Marketing Research Request Form was explained previously, here we need only note that you put your industry and company designation as well as the year and quarter of your decision in the spaces provided at the top of the form. (If you are using the DSS Disk to enter your decisions, your designation and the year and quarter will automatically appear at the top of the form.) Your first decision, which is requesting marketing research information only, will be for Year 1, Quarter 0; and your second decision will be for Year 1, Quarter 1; and so on through the four quarters of each year. Your industry letter and company number will be provided by your instructor at the beginning of simulation play.

Enter the number of the research study in the appropriate space on the marketing research request form to purchase the desired research study. If you are using the DSS Disk, you will be prompted to enter the number of the research study you wish to buy and by entering that number(s) the computer will automatically toggle the N (for No) to a Y (for Yes). If you change your mind, simply enter the appropriate number once again to toggle the Y back to an

N. You may buy as many of the studies as you want (1 through 12), or none of them.

THE MANAGEMENT DECISION FORM

In completing the Management Decision Form you should first identify the year, quarter, industry, and company in the appropriate spaces at the top of the form. (Automatic if you're entering decisions on the DSS Disk.) For each of the models you market you will make a set of decisions. These must be recorded very carefully on the Marketing Management Decision Form for each quarter. Careless mistakes may cost you thousands of dollars.

To designate the TV model you wish to produce, place the model code (A, B, C, etc.) in the appropriate square opposite Model Code. The *order* in which you record your model is *very* important. If you select model D for your model 1 decision for your first decision (Year 1, Quarter 1), you must continue to record model D in the model 1 position. If you inadvertently move your models, the computer program will assume you have changed models! It is suggested that, when you make your first decision, **you** record the model codes in alphabetical order. Thereafter, it will be easy for you to remember the proper order of your model codes.

On the next line you enter your selling price to your dealers. The number of units of this model that you want to produce is indicated on the next line. On the next few lines indicate how much you wish to spend on each form of promotion for that particular TV model. Note that these amounts are in thousands of dollars. For example, if you want to spend $1000 on TV advertising, you simply enter a 1 in the space opposite TV Advertising. Complete the form in this manner for each of the TV models you market.

Next you determine the number of salespersons you would like calling on your dealers. If you are entering your decisions on the computer disk, the last set of decisions you made will appear and all you need do is change the values to reflect your new decisions. Therefore, the size of your sales force will always appear. This is important because if you are using the forms in Appendix C of this book, you will need to maintain your own record of former decisions. Imagine what would happen, for instance, if you had to make a decision and you weren't quite certain of the number of salespersons you entered the previous quarter. If you put down a value other than the identical number of current salespersons, you will either be firing or hiring salespersons! Make certain you maintain good records and refer to them when you are making decisions and entering data for new decisions.

Your next entry is for the amount, if any, you wish to invest in R & D. Note this entry is in thousands. If you enter a 100 you will have invested $100,000 in R & D for that quarter. You begin the simulation with 400 dealers, but you may reallocate those dealers any way you choose *at no expense* on the first decision only! Thereafter there is a dealer change expense whenever you add, delete, or shift dealers.

You should now be prepared to play **Marketing Simulation**. However, we would like to give you a few last pointers. Be very careful when completing your forms. Transposing digits and leaving spaces blank when you intended to complete them are two common mistakes that are very costly and can easily be avoided if you are careful. If you are using the blank forms at the back of this book, you should get a piece of carbon paper and make a duplicate of all the decisions you make. These records will be very important when you are making future decisions. Your instructor may not return your decision form once you hand it in. If you are entering your decisions via a computer directly on your DSS Disk, double check your entries to ensure they are correct. We recommend that you also make a written record of the decisions you enter on the DSS Disk.

Finally, **Marketing Simulation** can be a good learning experience and lots of fun if you follow our advice about organizing your team. First, be prepared. Know this book! Second, organize your decisions so that each team member is responsible for a particular decision (or group of decisions). If you have problems with team members not carrying out their fair share of the workload, try to work it out yourselves; seek advice from your instructor only if you cannot solve problems within the team.

Appendix C
Blank Forms

FORM 1
OBJECTIVES AND PLANNING FORM

Year _____   Industry (Letter) _____
Quarter _____   Company (Number) _____

1. What are your major objectives for the coming quarter? _____
   _____
   _____

2. What overall strategy have you planned to enable you to reach your objectives?
   _____
   _____
   _____

3. What specific tactics do you plan to implement to enable you to achieve your objectives?

   a. PRODUCT TACTICS – _____
      _____

   b. PRICE TACTICS – _____
      _____

   c. CHANNEL TACTICS – _____
      _____

   d. PROMOTION TACTICS – _____
      _____

   TO BE COMPLETED WHEN DECISION RESULTS HAVE BEEN RECEIVED

4. Did you realize your stated objectives? _____
   _____

   Why? _____
   _____

   Why not? _____
   _____

5. What changes in objectives, strategy, and/or tactics have you planned for the next quarter, and why? _____
   _____
   _____
   _____

FORM 1
OBJECTIVES AND PLANNING FORM

Year _____   Industry (Letter) _____

Quarter _____   Company (Number) _____

1. What are your major objectives for the coming quarter? _____
   _____
   _____

2. What overall strategy have you planned to enable you to reach your objectives?
   _____
   _____
   _____

3. What specific tactics do you plan to implement to enable you to achieve your objectives?

   a. PRODUCT TACTICS – _____
      _____

   b. PRICE TACTICS – _____
      _____

   c. CHANNEL TACTICS – _____
      _____

   d. PROMOTION TACTICS – _____
      _____

   TO BE COMPLETED WHEN DECISION RESULTS HAVE BEEN RECEIVED

4. Did you realize your stated objectives? _____
   _____

   Why? _____
   _____

   Why not? _____
   _____

5. What changes in objectives, strategy, and/or tactics have you planned for the next quarter, and why? _____
   _____
   _____
   _____

FORM 1
OBJECTIVES AND PLANNING FORM

Year _____   Industry (Letter) _____

Quarter _____   Company (Number) _____

1. What are your major objectives for the coming quarter? _____
   _____
   _____

2. What overall strategy have you planned to enable you to reach your objectives?
   _____
   _____
   _____

3. What specific tactics do you plan to implement to enable you to achieve your objectives?

   a. PRODUCT TACTICS – _____
      _____

   b. PRICE TACTICS – _____
      _____

   c. CHANNEL TACTICS – _____
      _____

   d. PROMOTION TACTICS – _____
      _____

   TO BE COMPLETED WHEN DECISION RESULTS HAVE BEEN RECEIVED

4. Did you realize your stated objectives? _____
   _____

   Why? _____
   _____

   Why not?_____
   _____

5. What changes in objectives, strategy, and/or tactics have you planned for the next quarter, and why? _____
   _____
   _____
   _____

FORM 1
OBJECTIVES AND PLANNING FORM

Year _____   Industry (Letter) _____

Quarter _____   Company (Number) _____

1. What are your major objectives for the coming quarter? _____
   _____
   _____

2. What overall strategy have you planned to enable you to reach your objectives?
   _____
   _____
   _____

3. What specific tactics do you plan to implement to enable you to achieve your objectives?

   a. PRODUCT TACTICS – _____
   _____

   b. PRICE TACTICS – _____
   _____

   c. CHANNEL TACTICS – _____
   _____

   d. PROMOTION TACTICS – _____
   _____

   TO BE COMPLETED WHEN DECISION RESULTS HAVE BEEN RECEIVED

4. Did you realize your stated objectives? _____
   _____

   Why? _____
   _____

   Why not? _____
   _____

5. What changes in objectives, strategy, and/or tactics have you planned for the next quarter, and why? _____
   _____
   _____
   _____
   _____

FORM 1
OBJECTIVES AND PLANNING FORM

Year _____   Industry (Letter) _____

Quarter _____   Company (Number) _____

1. What are your major objectives for the coming quarter? _____
   _____
   _____

2. What overall strategy have you planned to enable you to reach your objectives?
   _____
   _____
   _____

3. What specific tactics do you plan to implement to enable you to achieve your objectives?

   a. PRODUCT TACTICS – _____
   _____

   b. PRICE TACTICS – _____
   _____

   c. CHANNEL TACTICS – _____
   _____

   d. PROMOTION TACTICS – _____
   _____

   TO BE COMPLETED WHEN DECISION RESULTS HAVE BEEN RECEIVED

4. Did you realize your stated objectives? _____
   _____

   Why? _____
   _____

   Why not?_____
   _____

5. What changes in objectives, strategy, and/or tactics have you planned for the next quarter, and why? _____
   _____
   _____
   _____
   _____

FORM 1
OBJECTIVES AND PLANNING FORM

Year _____ Industry (Letter) _____

Quarter _____ Company (Number) _____

1. What are your major objectives for the coming quarter? _____
   _____
   _____

2. What overall strategy have you planned to enable you to reach your objectives?
   _____
   _____
   _____

3. What specific tactics do you plan to implement to enable you to achieve your objectives?

   a. PRODUCT TACTICS – _____
   _____

   b. PRICE TACTICS – _____
   _____

   c. CHANNEL TACTICS – _____
   _____

   d. PROMOTION TACTICS – _____
   _____

   TO BE COMPLETED WHEN DECISION RESULTS HAVE BEEN RECEIVED

4. Did you realize your stated objectives? _____
   _____

   Why? _____
   _____

   Why not? _____
   _____

5. What changes in objectives, strategy, and/or tactics have you planned for the next quarter, and why? _____
   _____
   _____
   _____

FORM 1
OBJECTIVES AND PLANNING FORM

Year _____   Industry (Letter) _____

Quarter _____   Company (Number) _____

1. What are your major objectives for the coming quarter? _____
   _____
   _____

2. What overall strategy have you planned to enable you to reach your objectives?
   _____
   _____
   _____

3. What specific tactics do you plan to implement to enable you to achieve your objectives?

   a. PRODUCT TACTICS – _____
      _____

   b. PRICE TACTICS – _____
      _____

   c. CHANNEL TACTICS – _____
      _____

   d. PROMOTION TACTICS – _____
      _____

   TO BE COMPLETED WHEN DECISION RESULTS HAVE BEEN RECEIVED

4. Did you realize your stated objectives? _____
   _____

   Why? _____
   _____

   Why not? _____
   _____

5. What changes in objectives, strategy, and/or tactics have you planned for the next quarter, and why? _____
   _____
   _____
   _____
   _____

FORM 1
OBJECTIVES AND PLANNING FORM

Year _____ Industry (Letter) _____

Quarter _____ Company (Number) _____

1. What are your major objectives for the coming quarter? _____

2. What overall strategy have you planned to enable you to reach your objectives? _____

3. What specific tactics do you plan to implement to enable you to achieve your objectives?

    a. PRODUCT TACTICS – _____

    b. PRICE TACTICS – _____

    c. CHANNEL TACTICS – _____

    d. PROMOTION TACTICS – _____

    TO BE COMPLETED WHEN DECISION RESULTS HAVE BEEN RECEIVED

4. Did you realize your stated objectives? _____

    Why? _____

    Why not? _____

5. What changes in objectives, strategy, and/or tactics have you planned for the next quarter, and why? _____

FORM 1
OBJECTIVES AND PLANNING FORM

Year _____   Industry (Letter) _____

Quarter _____   Company (Number) _____

1. What are your major objectives for the coming quarter? _____
   _____
   _____

2. What overall strategy have you planned to enable you to reach your objectives?
   _____
   _____
   _____

3. What specific tactics do you plan to implement to enable you to achieve your objectives?

   a.   PRODUCT TACTICS – _____
        _____

   b.   PRICE TACTICS – _____
        _____

   c.   CHANNEL TACTICS – _____
        _____

   d.   PROMOTION TACTICS – _____
        _____

   TO BE COMPLETED WHEN DECISION RESULTS HAVE BEEN RECEIVED

4. Did you realize your stated objectives? _____
   _____

   Why? _____
   _____

   Why not? _____
   _____

5. What changes in objectives, strategy, and/or tactics have you planned for the next quarter, and why? _____
   _____
   _____
   _____
   _____

FORM 1
OBJECTIVES AND PLANNING FORM

Year _____   Industry (Letter) _____

Quarter _____   Company (Number) _____

1. What are your major objectives for the coming quarter? _____
   _____
   _____

2. What overall strategy have you planned to enable you to reach your objectives?
   _____
   _____
   _____

3. What specific tactics do you plan to implement to enable you to achieve your objectives?

   a. PRODUCT TACTICS – _____
      _____

   b. PRICE TACTICS – _____
      _____

   c. CHANNEL TACTICS – _____
      _____

   d. PROMOTION TACTICS – _____
      _____

   TO BE COMPLETED WHEN DECISION RESULTS HAVE BEEN RECEIVED

4. Did you realize your stated objectives? _____
   _____

   Why? _____
   _____

   Why not? _____
   _____

5. What changes in objectives, strategy, and/or tactics have you planned for the next quarter, and why? _____
   _____
   _____
   _____

FORM 2
MARKETING SIMULATION
MARKETING RESEARCH REQUEST FORM

Industry (Letter): _____ Year _____

Company (Number): _____ Quarter _____

STUDY	COST	Y or N
1. Quarterly Sales Forecast by Submarket	$20,000	_____
2. Current Number of Dealers by Company	$5,000	_____
3. Current Number of Dealers by Channel Type per Company	$20,000	_____
4. Current Promotion Expenditures by Company	$5,000	_____
5. Current Promotion Expenditures by Submarket per Company	$20,000	_____
6. Current Promotion Expenditures/Submarket/Medium/Company	$25,000	_____
7. Sales Force Size by Company	$15,000	_____
8. Cumulative Research & Development Expenditures /Company	$5,000	_____
9. Consumer Preference Study of All Models in Submarket 1	$30,000	_____
10. Consumer Preference Study of All Models in Submarket 2	$30,000	_____
11. Consumer Preference Study of All Models in Submarket 3	$30,000	_____
12. Consumer Preference Study of All Models in Submarket 4	$30,000	_____

Total: _____

FORM 3
MARKETING SIMULATION
MANAGEMENT DECISION FORM

Industry (Letter) _____   Year _____
Company (Number) _____   Quarter _____

	Model 1	Model 2	Model 3	Model 4
1. Model Code:	_____	_____	_____	_____
2. Price:	_____	_____	_____	_____
3. Units Produced:	_____	_____	_____	_____
4. TV Advertising (000):	_____	_____	_____	_____
5. Magazine Advertising (000):	_____	_____	_____	_____
6. Newspaper Advertising (000):	_____	_____	_____	_____
7. Sales Promotion (000):	_____	_____	_____	_____

8. Sales Force: _____

9. Research and Development (000): _____

	Furniture Store	Specialty Store	Discount Store	Department Store
10. Dealer Allocation:	_____	_____	_____	_____

FORM 2
MARKETING SIMULATION
MARKETING RESEARCH REQUEST FORM

Industry (Letter): _____   Year _____

Company (Number): _____   Quarter _____

STUDY	COST	Y or N
1. Quarterly Sales Forecast by Submarket	$20,000	_____
2. Current Number of Dealers by Company	$5,000	_____
3. Current Number of Dealers by Channel Type per Company	$20,000	_____
4. Current Promotion Expenditures by Company	$5,000	_____
5. Current Promotion Expenditures by Submarket per Company	$20,000	_____
6. Current Promotion Expenditures/Submarket/Medium/Company	$25,000	_____
7. Sales Force Size by Company	$15,000	_____
8. Cumulative Research & Development Expenditures /Company	$5,000	_____
9. Consumer Preference Study of All Models in Submarket 1	$30,000	_____
10. Consumer Preference Study of All Models in Submarket 2	$30,000	_____
11. Consumer Preference Study of All Models in Submarket 3	$30,000	_____
12. Consumer Preference Study of All Models in Submarket 4	$30,000	_____

=====

Total:

**FORM 3
MARKETING SIMULATION
MANAGEMENT DECISION FORM**

Industry (Letter) ____ Year ____

Company (Number) ____ Quarter ____

	Model 1	Model 2	Model 3	Model 4
1. Model Code:	____	____	____	____
2. Price:	____	____	____	____
3. Units Produced:	____	____	____	____
4. TV Advertising (000):	____	____	____	____
5. Magazine Advertising (000):	____	____	____	____
6. Newspaper Advertising (000):	____	____	____	____
7. Sales Promotion (000):	____	____	____	____

8. Sales Force: ____

9. Research and Development (000): ____

	Furniture Store	Specialty Store	Discount Store	Department Store
10. Dealer Allocation:	____	____	____	____

FORM 2
MARKETING SIMULATION
MARKETING RESEARCH REQUEST FORM

Industry (Letter): ____   Year ____

Company (Number): ____   Quarter ____

STUDY	COST	Y or N
1. Quarterly Sales Forecast by Submarket	$20,000	_____
2. Current Number of Dealers by Company	$5,000	_____
3. Current Number of Dealers by Channel Type per Company	$20,000	_____
4. Current Promotion Expenditures by Company	$5,000	_____
5. Current Promotion Expenditures by Submarket per Company	$20,000	_____
6. Current Promotion Expenditures/Submarket/Medium/Company	$25,000	_____
7. Sales Force Size by Company	$15,000	_____
8. Cumulative Research & Development Expenditures /Company	$5,000	_____
9. Consumer Preference Study of All Models in Submarket 1	$30,000	_____
10. Consumer Preference Study of All Models in Submarket 2	$30,000	_____
11. Consumer Preference Study of All Models in Submarket 3	$30,000	_____
12. Consumer Preference Study of All Models in Submarket 4	$30,000	_____

=====

Total:

**FORM 3
MARKETING SIMULATION
MANAGEMENT DECISION FORM**

Industry (Letter) ____
Company (Number) ____

Year ____
Quarter ____

	Model 1	Model 2	Model 3	Model 4
1. Model Code:	____	____	____	____
2. Price:	____	____	____	____
3. Units Produced:	____	____	____	____
4. TV Advertising (000):	____	____	____	____
5. Magazine Advertising (000):	____	____	____	____
6. Newspaper Advertising (000):	____	____	____	____
7. Sales Promotion (000):	____	____	____	____

8. Sales Force: ____

9. Research and Development (000): ____

	Furniture Store	Specialty Store	Discount Store	Department Store
10. Dealer Allocation:	____	____	____	____

FORM 2
MARKETING SIMULATION
MARKETING RESEARCH REQUEST FORM

Industry (Letter): ____   Year ____

Company (Number): ____   Quarter ____

STUDY	COST	Y or N
1. Quarterly Sales Forecast by Submarket	$20,000	_____
2. Current Number of Dealers by Company	$5,000	_____
3. Current Number of Dealers by Channel Type per Company	$20,000	_____
4. Current Promotion Expenditures by Company	$5,000	_____
5. Current Promotion Expenditures by Submarket per Company	$20,000	_____
6. Current Promotion Expenditures/Submarket/Medium/Company	$25,000	_____
7. Sales Force Size by Company	$15,000	_____
8. Cumulative Research & Development Expenditures /Company	$5,000	_____
9. Consumer Preference Study of All Models in Submarket 1	$30,000	_____
10. Consumer Preference Study of All Models in Submarket 2	$30,000	_____
11. Consumer Preference Study of All Models in Submarket 3	$30,000	_____
12. Consumer Preference Study of All Models in Submarket 4	$30,000	_____

=====

Total: _____

**FORM 3
MARKETING SIMULATION
MANAGEMENT DECISION FORM**

Industry (Letter) ____　　　　　　　　　　　　　　　　　　　　　Year ____

Company (Number) ____　　　　　　　　　　　　　　　　　　　Quarter ____

	Model 1	Model 2	Model 3	Model 4
1. Model Code:	____	____	____	____
2. Price:	____	____	____	____
3. Units Produced:	____	____	____	____
4. TV Advertising (000):	____	____	____	____
5. Magazine Advertising (000):	____	____	____	____
6. Newspaper Advertising (000):	____	____	____	____
7. Sales Promotion (000):	____	____	____	____

8. Sales Force: ____

9. Research and Development (000): ____

	Furniture Store	Specialty Store	Discount Store	Department Store
10. Dealer Allocation:	_____	_____	_____	_____

FORM 2
MARKETING SIMULATION
MARKETING RESEARCH REQUEST FORM

Industry (Letter): _____   Year _____

Company (Number): _____   Quarter _____

STUDY	COST	Y or N
1. Quarterly Sales Forecast by Submarket	$20,000	_____
2. Current Number of Dealers by Company	$5,000	_____
3. Current Number of Dealers by Channel Type per Company	$20,000	_____
4. Current Promotion Expenditures by Company	$5,000	_____
5. Current Promotion Expenditures by Submarket per Company	$20,000	_____
6. Current Promotion Expenditures/Submarket/Medium/Company	$25,000	_____
7. Sales Force Size by Company	$15,000	_____
8. Cumulative Research & Development Expenditures /Company	$5,000	_____
9. Consumer Preference Study of All Models in Submarket 1	$30,000	_____
10. Consumer Preference Study of All Models in Submarket 2	$30,000	_____
11. Consumer Preference Study of All Models in Submarket 3	$30,000	_____
12. Consumer Preference Study of All Models in Submarket 4	$30,000	_____

=====

Total: _____

FORM 3
MARKETING SIMULATION
MANAGEMENT DECISION FORM

Industry (Letter) ____ Year ____
Company (Number) ____ Quarter ____

	Model 1	Model 2	Model 3	Model 4
1. Model Code:	____	____	____	____
2. Price:	____	____	____	____
3. Units Produced:	____	____	____	____
4. TV Advertising (000):	____	____	____	____
5. Magazine Advertising (000):	____	____	____	____
6. Newspaper Advertising (000):	____	____	____	____
7. Sales Promotion (000):	____	____	____	____

8. Sales Force: ____

9. Research and Development (000): ____

	Furniture Store	Specialty Store	Discount Store	Department Store
10. Dealer Allocation:	____	____	____	____

FORM 2
MARKETING SIMULATION
MARKETING RESEARCH REQUEST FORM

Industry (Letter): _____   Year _____

Company (Number): _____   Quarter _____

STUDY	COST	Y or N
1. Quarterly Sales Forecast by Submarket	$20,000	_____
2. Current Number of Dealers by Company	$5,000	_____
3. Current Number of Dealers by Channel Type per Company	$20,000	_____
4. Current Promotion Expenditures by Company	$5,000	_____
5. Current Promotion Expenditures by Submarket per Company	$20,000	_____
6. Current Promotion Expenditures/Submarket/Medium/Company	$25,000	_____
7. Sales Force Size by Company	$15,000	_____
8. Cumulative Research & Development Expenditures /Company	$5,000	_____
9. Consumer Preference Study of All Models in Submarket 1	$30,000	_____
10. Consumer Preference Study of All Models in Submarket 2	$30,000	_____
11. Consumer Preference Study of All Models in Submarket 3	$30,000	_____
12. Consumer Preference Study of All Models in Submarket 4	$30,000	_____

=====

Total: _____

FORM 3
MARKETING SIMULATION
MANAGEMENT DECISION FORM

Industry (Letter) ____ Year ____
Company (Number) ____ Quarter ____

	Model 1	Model 2	Model 3	Model 4
1. Model Code:	____	____	____	____
2. Price:	____	____	____	____
3. Units Produced:	____	____	____	____
4. TV Advertising (000):	____	____	____	____
5. Magazine Advertising (000):	____	____	____	____
6. Newspaper Advertising (000):	____	____	____	____
7. Sales Promotion (000):	____	____	____	____

8. Sales Force: ____

9. Research and Development (000): ____

	Furniture Store	Specialty Store	Discount Store	Department Store
10. Dealer Allocation:	_____	_____	_____	_____

**FORM 2
MARKETING SIMULATION
MARKETING RESEARCH REQUEST FORM**

Industry (Letter): _____   Year _____
Company (Number): _____   Quarter _____

STUDY	COST	Y or N
1. Quarterly Sales Forecast by Submarket	$20,000	_____
2. Current Number of Dealers by Company	$5,000	_____
3. Current Number of Dealers by Channel Type per Company	$20,000	_____
4. Current Promotion Expenditures by Company	$5,000	_____
5. Current Promotion Expenditures by Submarket per Company	$20,000	_____
6. Current Promotion Expenditures/Submarket/Medium/Company	$25,000	_____
7. Sales Force Size by Company	$15,000	_____
8. Cumulative Research & Development Expenditures /Company	$5,000	_____
9. Consumer Preference Study of All Models in Submarket 1	$30,000	_____
10. Consumer Preference Study of All Models in Submarket 2	$30,000	_____
11. Consumer Preference Study of All Models in Submarket 3	$30,000	_____
12. Consumer Preference Study of All Models in Submarket 4	$30,000	_____

=====

Total: _____

**FORM 3
MARKETING SIMULATION
MANAGEMENT DECISION FORM**

Industry (Letter) _____ Year _____
Company (Number) _____ Quarter _____

	Model 1	Model 2	Model 3	Model 4
1. Model Code:	_____	_____	_____	_____
2. Price:	_____	_____	_____	_____
3. Units Produced:	_____	_____	_____	_____
4. TV Advertising (000):	_____	_____	_____	_____
5. Magazine Advertising (000):	_____	_____	_____	_____
6. Newspaper Advertising (000):	_____	_____	_____	_____
7. Sales Promotion (000):	_____	_____	_____	_____

8. Sales Force: _____

9. Research and Development (000): _____

	Furniture Store	Specialty Store	Discount Store	Department Store
10. Dealer Allocation:	_____	_____	_____	_____

FORM 2
MARKETING SIMULATION
MARKETING RESEARCH REQUEST FORM

Industry (Letter): _____   Year _____

Company (Number): _____   Quarter _____

STUDY	COST	Y or N
1. Quarterly Sales Forecast by Submarket	$20,000	_____
2. Current Number of Dealers by Company	$5,000	_____
3. Current Number of Dealers by Channel Type per Company	$20,000	_____
4. Current Promotion Expenditures by Company	$5,000	_____
5. Current Promotion Expenditures by Submarket per Company	$20,000	_____
6. Current Promotion Expenditures/Submarket/Medium/Company	$25,000	_____
7. Sales Force Size by Company	$15,000	_____
8. Cumulative Research & Development Expenditures /Company	$5,000	_____
9. Consumer Preference Study of All Models in Submarket 1	$30,000	_____
10. Consumer Preference Study of All Models in Submarket 2	$30,000	_____
11. Consumer Preference Study of All Models in Submarket 3	$30,000	_____
12. Consumer Preference Study of All Models in Submarket 4	$30,000	_____

=====

Total:

FORM 3
MARKETING SIMULATION
MANAGEMENT DECISION FORM

Industry (Letter) _____   Year _____
Company (Number) _____   Quarter _____

	Model 1	Model 2	Model 3	Model 4
1. Model Code:	A	E	J	N
2. Price:	180	225	3125	1000
3. Units Produced:	1260	2630	3010	700
4. TV Advertising (000):	_____	_____	_____	_____
5. Magazine Advertising (000):	_____	_____	_____	_____
6. Newspaper Advertising (000):	_____	_____	_____	_____
7. Sales Promotion (000):	_____	_____	_____	_____

8. Sales Force: _____

9. Research and Development (000): _____

	Furniture Store	Specialty Store	Discount Store	Department Store
10. Dealer Allocation:	_____	_____	_____	_____

FORM 4
PROFIT PLANNING FORM

Company =====> ?
Year =====> ?
Quarter =====> ?

FORECAST SALES

Model	Units	Price/Unit	Total
?	0	$0	$0
?	0	$0	$0
?	0	$0	$0
?	0	$0	$0

GROSS SALES =======> $0

COST OF SALES

Model	Units	Cost/Unit	Total	
?	0	$0	$0	$0
?	0	$0	$0	$0
?	0	$0	$0	$0
?	0	$0	$0	$0

COST OF SALES =====> $0

GROSS MARGIN =========> $0

OPERATING EXPENSES

Promotion	$0
Dealer Expense	$0
Dealer Change Expense	$0
Sales Force	$0
Research and Development	$0
Model Change Expense	$0
Administration	$20,000
Depreciation	$24,000
Interest Charge	$0

TOTAL OPERATING
EXPENSES ==============> $44,000

INCOME BEFORE TAXES ==========>   ($44,000)
TAXES (50%) ===================> $0

INCOME AFTER TAXES ===========>   ($44,000)

EARNINGS PER SHARE (EPS)   ($0.44)

FORM 5
RESEARCH AND DEVELOPMENT
EXPENDITURE FORM

Industry (Letter) _____

Company (Number) _____

		R & D Expenditures This Quarter	Cumulative R & D Expenditures
Year_____	Quarter_____	_____	_____
Year_____	Quarter_____	_____	_____
Year_____	Quarter_____	_____	_____
Year_____	Quarter_____	_____	_____
Year_____	Quarter_____	_____	_____
Year_____	Quarter_____	_____	_____
Year_____	Quarter_____	_____	_____
Year_____	Quarter_____	_____	_____
Year_____	Quarter_____	_____	_____
Year_____	Quarter_____	_____	_____
Year_____	Quarter_____	_____	_____
Year_____	Quarter_____	_____	_____
Year_____	Quarter_____	_____	_____
Year_____	Quarter_____	_____	_____
Year_____	Quarter_____	_____	_____
Year_____	Quarter_____	_____	_____
Year_____	Quarter_____	_____	_____
Year_____	Quarter_____	_____	_____
Year_____	Quarter_____	_____	_____

FORM 6
SOURCES AND USES OF FUNDS ANALYSIS

Company =====> ?
Year =====> ?
Quarter =====> ?

		Amount
SOURCES:	Cash (Current Balance)	$0
	Gross Sales	$0
	TOTAL SOURCES OF FUNDS	$0
USES:	Current Production	$0
	Overtime Production	$0
	Storage Charge	$0
	Promotion	$0
	Sales Force Expense	$0
	Dealer Expense	$0
	Dealer Change Expense	$0
	Marketing Research	$0
	Research and Development	$0
	Model Change Expense	$0
	Administration	$20,000
	Interest Expense	$0
	Income Taxes	$0
	TOTAL USE OF FUNDS	$0
	============	
	TOTAL CASH AVAILABLE	($20,000)

FORM 7
BREAK-EVEN ANALYSIS FORM

PRODUCT .... B
TOTAL FIXED COSTS FOR THE QUARTER.......................... $597,000
PERCENT ALLOCATED TO PRODUCT... 7%
ALLOCATED FIXED COSTS FOR THIS PRODUCT $41,790
VARIABLE COSTS PER UNIT $65
SELLING PRICE.. $395
CONTRIBUTION MARGIN.. $330

SENSITIVITY ANALYSIS   BREAK-EVEN ESTIMATES
ALTERNATIVE SELLING PRICES   PRICE   UNITS   DOLLARS

	Price	Units	Dollars
(10% Higher) ---->	$434.50	113	$49,141
(5% Higher) ---->	$414.75	119	$49,557
Specified Price====>	$395	127	$50,021
(5% Lower) ---->	$375.25	135	$50,545
(10% Lower) ---->	$355.50	144	$51,141

FORM 8
EXAMPLE OF A SALES FORECAST

SALES FORECAST FOR MODEL NUMBER 1

Year	--------------- Year 1 -------------	------
Quarter	1 2 3 4	5
ACTUAL UNIT SALES	250 350 500 750	1000
AVERAGE PERCENT GROWTH	NA NA 490 707	1082
DIFFERENCE	NA NA 10 43	(82)

NOTE: "NA" MEANS FORECAST IS UNAVAILABLE DUE TO INSUFFICIENT NUMBER OF PAST QUARTERS. A MINIMUM OF TWO QUARTERS IS NECESSARY FOR THIS FORECAST METHOD.

FORM 9
DISTRIBUTION EXPENSE PLANNING FORM

Company =====> 1
Year =====> 3
Quarter =====> 1

STORE TYPE	Last	QUARTER This	Shift
Furniture	40	50	10
TV	160	155	5
Discount	80	85	5
Department	120	120	0
Totals	400	410	20

Net Change in # Dealers = 10 $5,000 Dealer Add and/or Delete Expense (@$500)
Net Shift in Dealers = 10 $5,000 Dealer Shift Expense (@$500)
                                           $10,000 DEALER CHANGE EXPENSE

                                           $51,250 DEALER EXPENSE (# Dealers X $125)
                                           $61,250 TOTAL DISTRIBUTION EXPENSE

Appendix D
Sample Printouts

INCOME STATEMENT
INDUSTRY C - COMPANY 1
YEAR 3 - QUARTER 1
PROFESSOR BURNS
CLASS MARKETING

PAGE 1

SALES:
A	....	116280
E	....	164560
M	....	404125
R	....	370500

GROSS SALES   1055465

COST OF SALES:	A	E	M	R	
BEGINNING INVENTORY	0	0	0	0	
CURRENT PRODUCTION	51000	70200	300000	300000	
OVERTIME PRODUCTION	0	0	5500	0	
STORAGE CHARGE	498	144	0	750	
AVAILABLE FOR SALE	51498	70344	305500	300750	
ENDING INVENTORY	9960	2880	0	15000	
COST OF SALES	41538	67464	305500	285750	700252

GROSS MARGIN   355213

OPERATING EXPENSES

PROMOTIONS	67000	
DEALER EXPENSE	50000	
DEALER CHANGE EXPENSE	0	
PERSONAL SELLING	90000	
MARKETING RESEARCH	25000	
RESEARCH AND DEVELOPMENT	15000	
MODEL CHANGE EXPENSE	0	
ADMINISTRATION	20000	
DEPRECIATION	24000	
INTEREST CHARGE	0	291000

INCOME BEFORE TAXES   64213

INCOME TAX   32106

INCOME AFTER TAXES   32106

EARNINGS PER SHARE   0.321

RATIO ANALYSIS

		YOUR FIRM	INDUSTRY AVERAGE
PROFIT TO SALES RATIO	(NET PROFIT/SALES)	0.03042	-0.04342
SALES TO ASSETS TURNOVER	(SALES/ASSETS)	0.78760	1.01960
RETURN ON ASSETS	(NET PROFITS/TOTAL ASSETS)	0.02396	0.02631
RETURN ON NET WORTH	(NET PROFITS/NEW WORTH)	0.02396	0.24428

BALANCE SHEET
INDUSTRY C - COMPANY 1
YEAR 3 - QUARTER 1
PROFESSOR BURNS
CLASS MARKETING

ASSETS

CASH	228266
INVENTORY	27840
NET PLANT AND EQUIPMENT	1084000
TOTAL ASSETS	1340107

LIABILITIES AND OWNERS EQUITY

ACCOUNTS PAYABLE	0
CAPITAL STOCK (1$ PAR VALUE)	100000
RETAINED EARNINGS	1240107
TOTAL LIABILITIES AND OWNERS EQUITY	1340107

PROFIT ANALYSIS

MODEL	GROSS MARGIN PER UNIT	OPERATING EXPENSES PER UNIT	PROFIT PER UNIT	SALES UNITS	% OF TOTAL DOLLAR SALES
A	109.2719	71.1666	38.1053	684.	11.02
E	129.8075	81.4497	48.3578	748.	15.59
M	64.6721	61.4865	3.1856	1525.	38.29
R	297.3684	307.4763	-10.1079	285.	35.10

INVENTORY ANALYSIS

MODEL	A	E	M	R
BEGINNING INVENTORY	0	0	0	0
CURRENT PRODUCTION	850	780	1500	300
OVERTIME PRODUCTION	0	0	25	0
AVAILABLE FOR SALE	850	780	1525	300
LESS SALES	684	748	1525	285
ENDING INVENTORY	166	32	0	15

SALES INFORMATION PAGE 3
INDUSTRY C - COMPANY 1
YEAR 3 - QUARTER 1
PROFESSOR BURNS
CLASS MARKETING

UNIT SALES AND MARKET SHARE

SUBMARKET 1

COMPANY	PRODUCT	PRICE	FURNITURE UNITS	%	TV-SP UNITS	%	DISCOUNT UNITS	%	DEPARTMENT UNITS	%	TOTAL UNITS	MARKET SHARE %
1	A	170	101	20.7	329	16.9	84	8.6	170	11.6	684	14.1
2	D	145	87	17.8	591	30.3	246	25.3	318	21.8	1242	25.5
4	A	0	195	40.0	749	38.4	0	0.0	503	34.5	1447	29.7
5	B	250	105	21.5	279	14.3	642	66.0	469	32.1	1495	30.7

SUBMARKET 2

COMPANY	PRODUCT	PRICE	FURNITURE UNITS	%	TV-SP UNITS	%	DISCOUNT UNITS	%	DEPARTMENT UNITS	%	TOTAL UNITS	MARKET SHARE %
1	E	220	117	14.9	347	11.1	92	5.9	192	8.2	748	9.5
2	H	220	81	10.3	510	16.3	220	14.0	294	12.5	1105	14.1
3	H	250	108	13.7	548	17.5	262	16.7	344	14.6	1262	16.1
3	G	230	112	14.2	568	18.1	272	17.4	357	15.2	1309	16.7
4	G	215	245	31.2	864	27.5	0	0.0	622	26.4	1731	22.1
5	G	300	124	15.8	302	9.6	720	46.0	543	23.1	1689	21.5

SUBMARKET 3

COMPANY	PRODUCT	PRICE	FURNITURE UNITS	%	TV-SP UNITS	%	DISCOUNT UNITS	%	DEPARTMENT UNITS	%	TOTAL UNITS	MARKET SHARE %
1	M	265	231	19.8	699	15.0	199	8.5	396	11.4	1525	13.1
2	M	270	107	9.2	680	14.6	316	13.6	401	11.5	1504	12.9
3	K	250	176	15.1	909	19.5	468	20.1	584	16.8	2137	18.4
3	M	330	129	11.1	667	14.3	343	14.7	428	12.3	1567	13.5
4	K	290	364	31.3	1305	28.1	0	0.0	960	27.5	2629	22.6
5	K	375	157	13.5	390	8.4	1001	43.0	718	20.6	2266	19.5

SUBMARKET 4

COMPANY	PRODUCT	PRICE	FURNITURE UNITS	%	TV-SP UNITS	%	DISCOUNT UNITS	%	DEPARTMENT UNITS	%	TOTAL UNITS	MARKET SHARE %
1	R	1300	42	15.4	143	13.2	32	5.9	68	8.4	285	10.5
2	P	800	34	12.5	246	22.8	89	16.5	122	15.0	491	18.2
4	P	0	119	43.8	479	44.4	0	0.0	296	36.5	894	33.1
5	P	900	76	27.9	211	19.5	420	77.8	326	40.1	1033	38.2

YOUR CUMMULATIVE R+D EXPENDITURES ARE   134200.   YOUR R+D INDEX IS 115

EARNINGS PER SHARE BY COMPANY

COMPANY	QUARTER	GAME
1	0.32	1.61
2	0.24	2.04
3	1.28	6.01
4	-1.09	- 5.77
5	5.82	- 7.91

MARKETING RESEARCH RESULTS   PAGE   4
INDUSTRY C - COMPANY 1
YEAR 3 - QUARTER 1
PROFESSOR BURNS
CLASS MARKETING

ESTIMATED SALES FOR YEAR 3 QUARTER 2

SUBMARKET 1	5481.
SUBMARKET 2	8830.
SUBMARKET 3	13093.
SUBMARKET 4	3045.

NUMBER OF DEALERS BY COMPANY

COMPANY	DEALERS
1	400.
2	400.
3	470.
4	355.
5	400.

NUMBER OF DEALERS BY CHANNEL BY COMPANY

COMPANY	FURNITURE	TV-SP	DISCOUNT	DEPARTMENT
1	80	160	40	120
2	35	165	75	125
3	50	180	90	150
4	75	140	0	140
5	30	70	170	130

PROMOTION EXPENDITURES BY COMPANY

COMPANY	EXPENDITURES
1	67000
2	116000
3	121000
4	135000
5	147000

PROMOTION EXPENDITURES BY SUBMARKET BY COMPANY

COMPANY	SUBMARKET 1	SUBMARKET 2	SUBMARKET 3	SUBMARKET 4
1	24000	26000	8000	9000
2	23000	29000	29000	35000
3	0	59000	62000	0
4	0	62000	73000	0
5	36000	37000	37000	37000

PROMOTION EXPENDITURES BY SUBMARKET BY MEDIUM BY COMPANY

TV ADV

COMPANY	SUBMARKET 1	SUBMARKET 2	SUBMARKET 3	SUBMARKET 4
1	0	2000	2000	2000
2	6000	9000	9000	11000
3	0	18000	18000	0
4	0	17000	19000	0
5	14000	14000	14000	14000

MAGAZINE ADV

COMPANY	SUBMARKET 1	SUBMARKET 2	SUBMARKET 3	SUBMARKET 4
1	11000	2000	2000	2000
2	4000	6000	5000	8000
3	0	5000	9000	0
4	0	15000	17000	0
5	7000	7000	7000	7000

NEWSPAPER ADV

COMPANY	SUBMARKET 1	SUBMARKET 2	SUBMARKET 3	SUBMARKET 4
1	13000	11000	2000	2000
2	7000	6000	6000	7000
3	0	24000	20000	0
4	0	12000	15000	0
5	7000	7000	7000	7000

SALES PROMOTION

COMPANY	SUBMARKET 1	SUBMARKET 2	SUBMARKET 3	SUBMARKET 4
1	0	11000	2000	3000
2	6000	8000	9000	9000
3	0	12000	15000	0
4	0	18000	22000	0
5	8000	9000	9000	9000

CUMMULATIVE RESEARCH AND DEVELOPMENT EXPENDITURES BY COMPANY

COMPANY	EXPENDITURES
1	134200.
2	40000.
3	420000.
4	430000.
5	0.

PRODUCT PREFERENCE RATINGS FOR SUBMARKET 1
54% PREFERRED PRODUCT A TO PRODUCT B
55% PREFERRED PRODUCT A TO PRODUCT C
52% PREFERRED PRODUCT A TO PRODUCT D
46% PREFERRED PRODUCT B TO PRODUCT A
51% PREFERRED PRODUCT B TO PRODUCT C
48% PREFERRED PRODUCT B TO PRODUCT D
45% PREFERRED PRODUCT C TO PRODUCT A
49% PREFERRED PRODUCT C TO PRODUCT B
47% PREFERRED PRODUCT C TO PRODUCT D
48% PREFERRED PRODUCT D TO PRODUCT A
52% PREFERRED PRODUCT D TO PRODUCT B
53% PREFERRED PRODUCT D TO PRODUCT C

PRODUCT PREFERENCE RATINGS FOR SUBMARKET 2
64% PREFERRED PRODUCT E TO PRODUCT F
60% PREFERRED PRODUCT E TO PRODUCT G
52% PREFERRED PRODUCT E TO PRODUCT H
36% PREFERRED PRODUCT F TO PRODUCT E
45% PREFERRED PRODUCT F TO PRODUCT G
38% PREFERRED PRODUCT F TO PRODUCT H
40% PREFERRED PRODUCT G TO PRODUCT E
55% PREFERRED PRODUCT G TO PRODUCT F
42% PREFERRED PRODUCT G TO PRODUCT H
48% PREFERRED PRODUCT H TO PRODUCT E
63% PREFERRED PRODUCT H TO PRODUCT F
58% PREFERRED PRODUCT H TO PRODUCT G

PRODUCT PREFERENCE RATINGS FOR SUBMARKET 3
64% PREFERRED PRODUCT J TO PRODUCT K
52% PREFERRED PRODUCT J TO PRODUCT L
55% PREFERRED PRODUCT J TO PRODUCT M
36% PREFERRED PRODUCT K TO PRODUCT J
38% PREFERRED PRODUCT K TO PRODUCT L
41% PREFERRED PRODUCT K TO PRODUCT M
48% PREFERRED PRODUCT L TO PRODUCT J
63% PREFERRED PRODUCT L TO PRODUCT K
53% PREFERRED PRODUCT L TO PRODUCT M
45% PREFERRED PRODUCT M TO PRODUCT J
59% PREFERRED PRODUCT M TO PRODUCT K
47% PREFERRED PRODUCT M TO PRODUCT L

PRODUCT PREFERENCE RATINGS FOR SUBMARKET 4
55% PREFERRED PRODUCT N TO PRODUCT P
54% PREFERRED PRODUCT N TO PRODUCT R
52% PREFERRED PRODUCT N TO PRODUCT S
45% PREFERRED PRODUCT P TO PRODUCT N
49% PREFERRED PRODUCT P TO PRODUCT R
47% PREFERRED PRODUCT P TO PRODUCT S
46% PREFERRED PRODUCT R TO PRODUCT N
51% PREFERRED PRODUCT R TO PRODUCT P
48% PREFERRED PRODUCT R TO PRODUCT S
48% PREFERRED PRODUCT S TO PRODUCT N
53% PREFERRED PRODUCT S TO PRODUCT P
52% PREFERRED PRODUCT S TO PRODUCT R

Appendix E
Sample Tests

PART I: MULTIPLE CHOICE

_____ 1. The setting for this simulation game is the

   a. fashion industry.
   b. TV industry.
   c. fast-food industry.
   d. automobile industry.

_____ 2. Each industry in this marketing simulation game may include up to

   a. 2 firms.
   b. 3 firms.
   c. 4 firms.
   d. 5 firms.
   e. 6 firms.

_____ 3. Objectives should be

   a. specific and related to a particular result.
   b. reasonable and flexible.
   c. written down.
   d. all of the above.

_____ 4. The statement that reflects a company's financial position at a given point in time is the

   a. income statement.
   b. balance sheet.
   c. inventory analysis.
   d. profit analysis.

5. The main yardstick you should use to compare your quarterly profit standing with your competitors' is

   a. the R & D index.
   b. market share.
   c. gross sales.
   d. EPS.

6. Determining the firm's marketing strategy involves setting a plan for the variables of

   a. product.
   b. price.
   c. promotion.
   d. distribution.
   e. selecting a target market.
   f. all of the above.

7. Overall plans for accomplishing objectives are

   a. tactics.
   b. policies.
   c. strategies.
   d. none of the above.

8. The number of outstanding shares of common stock in this game is

   a. 250,000.
   b. 300,000.
   c. 125,000.
   d. 100,000.

9. The per-quarter interest rate on bank loans is

   a. 12 percent.
   b. 9 percent.
   c. 16 percent.
   d. 4 percent.

10. Each firm must produce a minimum of

    a. 1000 TV sets per quarter.
    b. 2000 TV sets per quarter.
    c. 3000 TV sets per quarter.
    d. 4000 TV sets per quarter.

11. All TV models in this game include

    a. a VHF/UHF channel dial.
    b. a VHF/UHF antenna.
    c. remote control.
    d. all of the above.
    e. (a) and (b) only.

12. The production costs for the various models range from

    a. $50 to $300.
    b. $60 to $1000.
    c. $75 to $250.
    d. $60 to $1500.

13. Your company can change models

    a. at the beginning of a new quarter.
    b. at the beginning of a year.
    c. at any time.
    d. none of the above.

14. The total cost to change a model is

    a. $60,000 per model changed.
    b. $50,000 per model changed.
    c. $25,000 per model changed.
    d. none of the above.

15. The overtime charge to produce more models is

    a. 10 percent of production cost.
    b. 15 percent of production cost.
    c. 20 percent of production cost.
    d. 5 percent of production cost.

16. Production should be scheduled so that

    a. fewer models are available for sale than the quantity forecast.
    b. more models are available for sale than the quantity forecast.
    c. the number of models available for sale is equal to the quantity forecast.

17. If model B has a beginning inventory of 400 units and the sales forecast is 2200 units, the amount in current production should be

    a. 2600 units.
    b. 2200 units.
    c. 1800 units.
    d. 1400 units.

18. The types of dealers that may be used in this game are

    a. furniture stores.
    b. discount stores.
    c. department stores.
    d. TV specialty stores.
    e. all of the above.

132   Marketing Simulation

_____   19. The cost to add, drop, or shift a dealer is

   a. $200.
   b. $300.
   c. $400.
   d. none of the above.

_____   20. Some pricing objectives that a firm may set are the following:

   a. achieve a target return on net sales or investment.
   b. maintain or improve market share.
   c. meet competition.
   d. all of the above.
   e. (a) and (b) only.

_____   21. A form of analysis that tells you how many units must be sold at a particular price to just cover fixed and variable costs (total costs) is:

   a. profit planning.
   b. contribution pricing.
   c. break-even analysis.
   d. exponential smoothing.

_____   22. The part on your computer disk that is used to input your research and management decisions quarter to quarter is:

   a. MIS.
   b. DIS.
   c. MESS.
   d. DSS.

_____   23. The way in which your team's decisions for a quarter are communicated to your instructor is:

   a. you write them down on notebook paper.
   b. you use forms purchased at your bookstore.
   c. you input them on your team DSS disk and hand it to your instructor.
   d. each team member hands a DSS disk to your instructor.

_____   24. What must you copy onto your DSS disk in order for it to run the DIS?

   a. BASICA.
   b. Lotus 1-2-3.
   c. your team members' names.
   d. nothing, it will run without anything on it.

_____ 25. When your instructor returns your team DSS disk, how do you find out how your company did?

   a. he will tell you.
   b. ask your team members.
   c. print out the output file.
   d. all of the above.

PART II: TRUE–FALSE

_____ 1. This marketing simulation game requires a knowledge of computer operation on the part of the student.

_____ 2. The designation "A-4" represents the fourth company in industry A.

_____ 3. To establish a responsibility center you should make each team member responsible for a specific set of activities.

_____ 4. Records of past decisions are not important for making the best possible decisions.

_____ 5. A company's net worth is determined by subtracting its expenses from its sales.

_____ 6. The marketing research request form is always completed one quarter in advance of the time you need research information.

_____ 7. You may select as many as six TV models to market.

_____ 8. Only companies in the same industry actually compete with one another.

_____ 9. For greater success in your decision making you should use your own knowledge about the TV industry in addition to the description of the industry provided in this book.

_____ 10. Every company begins with identical operating revenues, costs, and profits.

_____ 11. The higher your profits, the higher your earnings per share.

____ 12. The balance sheet indicates the amounts of a company's assets and liabilities.

____ 13. Should your uses of cash exceed your sources of cash, your firm will automatically go bankrupt.

____ 14. Depreciation per quarter in this game is $24,000.

____ 15. There are six submarkets in this game.

____ 16. The production cost is the same for all models produced for the same submarket.

____ 17. It is possible to have a stock out in marketing simulation.

____ 18. It is not possible to purchase research data that forecast quarterly industry sales by submarket.

____ 19. An ending inventory will be stored at 10 percent of the production cost of each unit.

____ 20. The inventory analysis reports in terms of the dollar value of TV sets.

____ 21. Sales forecast studies are 100 percent accurate in this simulation game.

____ 22. A firm may spend money on research and development and not receive any significant benefit from this expense.

____ 23. Dealer maintenance expense per quarter is $150 per dealer.

____ 24. The price you set for your models is the price at which your models are sold to consumers.

____ 25. The R & D index provides a record of R & D expenditures.

____ 26. Ideally, dollars should be spent on promotion until marginal cost equals marginal revenue.

____ 27. There are no "lagged" effects of promotion in this game.

Appendix E   135

_____ 28. The "best" models to produce are those with the greatest consumer preference.

_____ 29. Income taxes in this game are 60 percent of before-tax profits.

_____ 30. Each firm begins this game with a market share of 20 percent (if there are 5 firms).

_____ 31. Sensitivity analysis helps you see the effects of alternative prices on the breakeven level for unit sales.

_____ 32. You definitely should not experiment with the DSS disk that comes with this book before your instructor tells you your company's designation.

_____ 33. The team DSS disk is the only one that should have your company's current history file on it throughout game play.

_____ 34. A decision support system world will characterize management decision making in the future.

_____ 35. With each new quarter of play, your decisions and results for last quarter will automatically be added to your company's history file on your team DSS disk.

ANSWERS

Part I: Multiple Choice

1.	B	(see page 2)
2.	D	(see page 2)
3.	D	(see page 11)
4.	B	(see page 13)
5.	D	(see page 23)
6.	F	(see page 25)
7.	C	(see page 25)
8.	D	(see page 24)
9.	D	(see page 23)
10.	B	(see page 33)
11.	E	(see page 31)
12.	B	(see page 33)
13.	B	(see page 31)
14.	D	(see page 31)
15.	A	(see page 38)
16.	C	(see page 39)
17.	C	(see page 38)
18.	E	(see page 44)
19.	D	(see page 44)
20.	D	(see page 47)
21.	C	(see page 49)
22.	B	(see page 4)
23.	C	(see page 7)
24.	A	(see page 4)
25.	C	(see page 7)

Part II: True–False

1.	F	(see Preface, page xi)
2.	T	(see page 8)
3.	T	(see page 9)
4.	F	(see page 9)
5.	F	(see page 22)
6.	T	(see page 57)
7.	F	(see page 38)
8.	T	(see page 2)
9.	F	(see page 1)
10.	T	(see page 21)
11.	T	(see page 23)
12.	T	(see page 23)
13.	F	(see page 23)
14.	T	(see page 24)
15.	F	(see page 28)
16.	F	(see page 33)
17.	F	(see page 40)
18.	F	(see page 58)
19.	F	(see page 38)
20.	F	(see page 39)
21.	F	(see page 25)
22.	T	(see page 41)

23.	F	(see page 45)
24.	F	(see page 48)
25.	F	(see page 42)
26.	T	(see page 52)
27.	F	(see page 55)
28.	T	(see page 30)
29.	F	(see page 23)
30.	T	(see page 5)
31.	T	(see page 70)
32.	F	(see page 20)
33.	F	(see page 71)
34.	T	(see page 3)
35.	T	(see page 68)

Appendix F
Installing Basic on Your DSS Disk

Market Simulation is written in BASIC, and it will operate as long as you are using any version of BASIC; however, you must copy BASIC onto your DSS disk because BASIC is licensed software.

To install BASIC on your Student DSS disk, you must first determine whether or not you have a compatible computer form of BASIC. To find out, list the BASIC file, using the DIR command, to see what it is called. Normally, the BASIC file is contained with DOS files. In some cases, you may have a separate disk containing the BASIC program for your machine. In any case, you will need to know what it is named since you will be copying the BASIC file to your DSS disk.

If it is called BASICA.COM, you have the version of BASIC that the **Marketing Simulation** program will look for when it is loaded. Now, all you need do is copy it directly onto the DSS disk. Put the source disk with BASICA.COM into Drive A, and place your DSS disk in Drive B. Assuming you already have DOS booted, type the following at the A:

COPY A:BASICA.COM B: (Press Return)

On the other hand, if your BASIC is called something else, perhaps "BASIC.EXE," or "GWBASIC.COM," or some other des–ig–na–tion, you will need to rename it so the **Marketing Simulation** program will be able to recognize it. To do this, suppose your version of BASIC is called BASIC.EXE. Put the source disk (with this version of BASIC you want to copy) in Drive A, and put your DSS disk in Drive B. Type the following at the A:

COPY A:BASIC.EXE B:BASICA.COM (Press Enter)

This accomplishes two things. First, it copies your version of BASIC onto the DSS disk and second it renames your BASIC file to the name, BASICA.COM, that **Marketing Simulation** needs in order to run.

If you are copying BASIC from a hard disk drive, it will be best to ask for help from someone who is familiar with the files on the hard disk drive you are using. He or she should be able to tell you how to address BASIC on the hard drive and copy it to your DSS disk.

To run your DIS part of your DSS, put your DSS disk with BASIC now properly copied on it in Drive A. Type the following at the A:

STUDENT (Press Enter)

The **Marketing Simulation** logo will appear, and you can follow the instructions on the screen to use the DIS. There is a menu item allowing you to execute the DAT part of **Marketing Simulation.**

Index

Balance sheet, 23-24
  example printout of, 24
  your company's, 23
BASIC, installing on DSS Disk, 139-140
Blank forms, 83-120
Borrowing, 77
  and automatic ash loans, 77
Break-Even Analysis Form (Form 7), 118
Cash requirements, 76-77
  and cash flow, 76-77
Changing models, 38
Channels. *See* Distribution
Competition, studies of, 58-61
Consumer preferences, 30-31
  changing of, 42-43
  studies of, 61
DAT
  how to operate, 71
  loading, 18-19
  running, 19-20
  sharing, 71-72
  tools, 69-70
Dealers. *See* Distribution
Decision Analysis Tools, 76-72
Decision Input System, 3-4, 16-18
Decision Support System, 3-4
Decisions
  completing decision forms for, 79-81
  in Marketing Simulation, 1
Depreciation, 75
DIS, 16-18
Disk Drive Assignment, 17-18
Distribution, 43-46
  adding dealers to, 45

  channel strategies for, 44
  and competitive dealer studies, 58-59
  and dealer allocation, 44-46
  and dealer maintenance, 45
  and distribution expense planning form (Form 9), 15, 120
  dropping dealers from, 46
  effects of competitors in, 46
  and examples of channels, 43
  and management decision forms, 45-46
  and shifting dealers, 45-46
  types of dealers in, 44
Earnings per share, 23
Environments changing, 4-5
Features of products, 31-33
Forecasting, 33-38
  research study, 35-36
  using DAT, 36-38
Income statement, 21-23, 73-76
  and available for sale, 75
  and cost of sales, 74-75
  and current production, 74
  and income and taxes, 76
  and operating expenses, 75-76
  and sales, 74
Industry (television), 21
Industry set-up, 16-17
Interest rate, 23, 77
Inventory, 38-41
  analysis of, 14
  available for sale in, 39-40
  beginning, 39-40

Inventory *(continued)*
  current production in, 39-40
  ending, 39-40
  and planning, 338
  and sales forecasts, 39
Loans, 23, 77
Management decision form (Form 3), 6, 13, 80-81
  blank forms of, 96-114
  how to complete, 80-81
Marketing Information System, 68-69
Marketing research, 47-62
  and competitive dealer studies, 58-59
  and competitive promotion studies, 59-60
  and competitive research and development studies, 60-61
  and competitive sales force studies, 60
  and consumer preference studies, 61-62
  and the quarterly sales forecast, 58
  request form (Form 2) for, 8, 12-13, 79-80, 95-113
  results printout form, 126-128
Marketing simulation
  channel strategy in, 44
  marketing research in, 57-62
  model selection in, 30-31
  pricing analysis in, 48-51
  product strategies in, 30-35
  profit analysis in, 14, 51
  profit planning in, 14-15, 50-51
  promotion strategy in, 54-55
  research and development in, 41-43
  sales forecasting in, 33-38
  setting for, 2-3
  submarkets in, 28-29
Markets
  consumer, 38
  industrial, 38
  and submarkets, 28-29
Market segmentation
  advantages of, 28
  disadvantages of, 28
  and submarket 1, 28
  and submarket 2, 29
  and submarket 3, 29
  and submarket 4, 29
Market share, 35
Models (television)
  changing of, 31, 38
  features on, 31-33
  on the model description chart, 33
  selection of, 30-31
Objectives
  company, 11
  objectives and planning form (Form 1), 12, 85-94
  pricing, 47
Operating expenses, 22, 75-76
Overtime costs, 38
Performance
  evaluation of, 63-67
Personal sales force
  salaries, 54
  size, 54
  study, 60
Practice Data Set (X-1), 71
Pricing, 47-51
  at the market, 48
  break-even analysis, 49-50
  considerations in, 47
  discount, 47
  objectives for, 47
  penetration, 57
  premium, 58
  profit analysis for, 51
  profit planning for, 50-51
Printer, 17-18
Printouts, examples of, 123-128
Product
  features for, 31-33
  and overtime costs, 38
  strategies for, 29-30
  strategies in Marketing Simulation, 30-43
Production capabilities and constraints, 38
  and minimum production, 38
  and the model change expense account, 38
  and model changes, 38
  and overtime, 38
  and production costs, 33

Product *(continued)*
   and quantities available for sale, 39
   and sales forecasting and production, 33-38
   and selecting television models, 30-31
   and storage costs, 38
Profit
   analysis, 51
   planning, 50-51
   profit planning form (Form 4), 115
Promotion
   budget for, 52-53
   communication in, 51
   and competitive promotion studies, 55, 59-60
   by fixed percentage of sales, 53
   to meet competition, 53
   promotion mix for, 52
   strategy for, 51-52
   by task or objective approach, 53
Research. *See* Marketing research
Research and development, 41-43
   and competitive studies, 60-61
   expenditure form (Form 5) for, 116
   expenditures on, 41
   index, 42
   messages, 14
Retained earnings, 23-24
Ratio analysis, 13
Sales information printout, 14, 125
Sales force, 54
Simulation, reasons for, 2
Sources and uses of funds and "cash flow," 76-77
   and the sources and uses of funds form (Form 6), 15, 117
Stock, outstanding shares of, 23-24
Storage costs, 38
Strategy, marketing, 25-26
   effects of competition on, 26-27
   and the marketing mix, 25-26
   marketing mix variables for, 26
   and tactics, 26
   and target markets, 25
   and your company, 26
Student DSS Disk, operating, 15
Taxes
   calculation of, 22-23
   and credits, 76
Team DSS Disk, 6-7
Team organization, 7-11
   and communications, 9
   and consistent effort, 10
   and designation of company identity, 8
   and responsibility centers, 9
   and review and control, 9-10
Technological breakthrough, 42
Tests on Marketing Simulation, 120-135
Utility Menu, 17-18
X-1, 4, 7, 71